MOMENTS OF TRUTH

Personal Stories of Discovery

compiled by Randy Revell
Founder, Context Associated

MOMENTS OF TRUTH

Personal Stories of Discovery

First Edition

Compiled by: Randy Revell
Founder
Context Associated

Published by: Context Associated
3851 Clay Street
San Francisco, CA 94118

www.contextassociated.com

ISBN 0-9659724-0-2

Printed in the United States of America.

Produced & distributed by **Context Associated**
order lines: 888-773-8355
order fax: 415-387-7753

Dedication

Each person's life has a unique purpose which can be discovered and actualized. Context Associated exists as an avenue for this exploration. We produce programs that assist people in finding more success in the work place, greater intimacy in their relationships, more clarity and better balance in their lives by discovering exactly what is most important to them.

I have the privilege of introducing to you 27 of Context Associated's finest people, people who are willing to share some of the humorous and touching moments of their lives as they continue to learn, and grow, and contribute to the community around them.

All of us have stories about our lives that we communicate to others in an attempt to share with them some aspect of ourselves. These stories also help define who we are and what we value. At Context Associated our leaders sometimes use stories from their lives to illustrate points during the courses. This book contains some of those stories.

Context Associated is people. It is about people, by people and for people. I dedicate this book to those countless people who want happier, more effective, meaningful, and fulfilled lives. You are why we do what we do.

W. Randall Revell
Founder

Table of Contents

INTRODUCTION
by Randy Revell

THE STORIES

CHOICE
by Judy Revell

AUTHENTICITY
by Michele McNickle

RELATIONSHIP
by Phil Holcomb

STRONG SUPPORT
by Kathleen Carie

SUPPORT NETWORK
by Joanne Kotjan

Table of Contents

Table of Contents

Table of Contents

THE STORY TELLERS

Table of Contents

RESOURCES

INTRODUCTION

by Randy Revell

Green and Growing

Picture a perfectly shaped, fragrant red apple at the peak of perfection. Many would agree that this is one of the world's great beauties. Yet, at this moment of great beauty, the process of decay has already begun.

The old saying goes, "When you're green, you're growing. When you're ripe, you're rotten." This applies equally to apples and human beings. To be "green" as a human is to continue learning. The current saying "Been there, done that, got the T-shirt" illustrates that decay has surely begun to set in.

Many people find the experience of being "green" to be particularly uncomfortable or unattractive once they've been away from it for awhile. There is an awkwardness during the learning process. It's uncool—unless you have made up your mind that it's cool—to be growing.

So it's hard for many people to see the value in continued learning. Yet it is this strategy that keeps decay away, and keeps the juices of life flowing.

The type of learning doesn't much matter. It could be learning a new manual skill like typing or playing a musical instrument. It could be work-related or have nothing to do with one's profession. It's the very act of learning that keeps you growing.

It takes resources—usually time, energy and money—to learn and grow. For most of us, these resources are precious, and we spend them as wisely as we can. If I'm interested in the highest return on the investment of my resources, there is one area of focus that will always yield the highest crop. That focus is learning more about myself. Let's go back to that beautiful apple for a moment: the more I know about growing apples, the better choices I make, and the more apples I produce. The same is true for me about my life. The better I know myself, the higher my level of overall effectiveness (the more fruit I produce). This is due to the increased accuracy of the choices I make.

There are numerous pressures on us from families, friends, employers, religious groups, governments and society to make certain choices. These pressures are so intense that it's easy to bow to them without considering if they are in our own best interest.

When my self-perception accurately matches who I really am, I make more effective choices. As a result of these choices, I participate in situations and in ways that are most appropriate for me, which greatly contributes to my continued growth and, coincidentally, to the lives of those around me.

If a person wants to live life to the fullest, and wants to make a big difference, he or she will commit to a life-long process of self-exploration. Ultimately, the life that is truly in one's own best interests is the one that will best serve one's family, friends, colleagues, and community.

Everything is Context Associated

How we see determines what is seen. Both beauty and ugliness are in the eye of the beholder. What we see must pass through our beliefs, attitudes, positions, points of view—our context. By the time it does, it is changed, and often to the point where another person might not even recognize it.

For example, a piece of jewelry worn on someone's tongue can be viewed with admiration or disgust. It depends on who is looking. Likewise, the optimist and pessimist live in very different worlds.

Just about everything in life is associated with our context. This becomes abundantly clear as we read the true stories in this book.

Each of the stories contains a point at which the teller changes his or her mind. They see their situations differently. They have what we call a "context shift." As a result, things work.

Our greatest gift is that of choice. We can use that gift to change how we see the content of our lives. Although changing one's mind is often an unconscious process, it can also be conscious. An act of conscious choice to see something differently is a skill that can be developed. It is also one of the most valuable skills we can possess. This is one of the skills we teach at Context Associated.

THE STORIES

It's All In Your Point of View

by Judy Revell

When we were first starting out, Randy, my husband, would be out of town often, mostly teaching. There would be some months he'd be gone every week of the month for five or six days at a time. I was a fairly young wife and mother. I had a lot of self-confidence, but it wasn't based on much evidence such as being asked to join Mensa, or being the belle of the ball, or anything tangible like that. What made my husband's travels seem particularly hard was that they usually included the weekends because the courses he taught would extend over Saturday and Sunday. I stayed home most of the time. In fact, I thought stay-at-home life had no equal to mine.

Many women didn't work for money or entertainment or for a reason like fulfillment then. It was the early seventies and the idea of fulfillment as a life goal was scarcely imagined by men or women. Most women didn't work outside of the home, especially if they were mothers. Some did, but most did not. I know I didn't. In fact, I quit my job as a stockbroker shortly after I became pregnant because. . . Well, I don't remember why anymore. I just did. I had a full-time job again only when our child was over nine years old. In other words, I couldn't count on work to fill any of my needs.

So what did I do? What any normal girl would have done. I cried a lot. I was unhappy when my husband was gone because he was gone. I was unhappy when he was at home because he had just been gone or was just going. It made perfect sense to me to be so gloomy.

To help rectify the situation I took classes such as basic photography and flower arranging. I could have told you about a lot of different subjects back then. Unfortunately, taking classes didn't work. I failed to increase the level of my happiness. After doing many different projects, and reading everything I could get my hands on about being happy, I was still very unhappy.

Finally what worked was that I changed my mind. I changed my mind about what was the source of my fulfillment. I changed my mind about how I felt about Randy being gone so often. It's still a mystery to me as to exactly what happened. After all, the truism is that people are supposed to be unhappy when the ones they care for are away. Instead, I changed my mind. I was happy when Randy was home, and happy when he wasn't. I gave up some good sympathy that way.

Changing my mind happened fast. It probably happened faster than writing this is taking. It took seconds, not days. First though, was deciding that I wanted to change my mind. What about me? What about my needs? Those were some of the questions that came up.

I decided that whether I felt happy and fulfilled was up to me. And I decided that I wanted to stay married to Randy, even though he was gone a lot of the time. I had fallen for him exactly the way he was, teacher and all. Granted, he had been on his most romantic behavior back then, and I had been with him much of the time when we were courting. Still, it was the decision of acceptance that made the biggest difference.

I'm glad I changed my mind.

Real Life

by Michele McNickle

I remember my first authentic moment. I was three years old and we were living in Waterford, Michigan. As my mother's first daughter, I was subject to occasional episodes of "dolling up." This particular day happened to be one of them. My mother dressed me in frilly white lace socks with underwear to match. On top of a frou-frou dress, this was just too much. Even at that age I had a sense of style and preference that did NOT include lace of any sort.

I also had a sense for creative solutions. I made my way to the patch of cement driveway between the house and the garage, and turned on the outdoor faucet to wet the cement. I then proceeded to walk vigorously back and forth, dragging my heels until I'd worked large enough holes in those socks to render them useless. Somehow I was much more pleased with my enthusiasm and determination than my mother.

By the seventh grade, my mother's ideas of fashion were much more appealing, simply because the goal of any seventh-grader was to be more grown-up, more acceptable, more "in." I had talked her into letting me get a pair of sandals with 5-inch heels! They were soooo cool, and so was I for wearing them. I borrowed a tee-shirt of Mom's with the French word "oui" across the front. I was the height of sophistication.

It didn't take long to find out just how chic I really was. As it turned out, "Oui" was also the name of a pornographic magazine. You can imagine how many boys at that age were anxious to give me this information. To make my day complete, the revered ninth graders didn't like my shoes either. I felt pretty small. From then on my life was about not creating any waves.

Remember the army slogan, "Be all that you can be"? Well, my slogan became "be all that they want you to be." I was willing to change my looks, beliefs and opinions to make myself acceptable. I expended an incredible amount of energy in my life in an attempt to be the most pleasing to the greatest number of people.

I turned my life around by investing in, rather than denying, myself. Enhancing my relationship with myself gave me a passion for authenticity. I now celebrate, love and accept myself, for the essence of who I am is quite wonderful. That doesn't mean there aren't issues or behaviors I'd still like to change, or that I'm not tempted to look outside of myself (to my job, my possessions, my partner) to define my self-worth. What it does mean is that I've seen what a dramatic difference it has made in my life to get behind who I am and use that momentum to create what I know is most important to me. Fully embracing myself has become one of the great challenges life has to offer. To be completely myself and have that be enough. The power of who I am does not lie in what I can do, (although I am one heck of a doer, just ask around!), it lies within—who I am at my core.

Each one of us is a gift, a unique contribution to the world that is only ours to give. Our task is to discover it, revel in it, celebrate its beauty, and commit to giving it fully and freely. That's what real living is all about.

Sara And Her Juice

by Phil Holcomb

Most people who talk to me about their relationships tell me that they know that how they feel about others is determined by how they feel about themselves. They also tell me that they forget this simple idea much more often than they remember it. Like just about every time a relationship is "not working." And, little wonder, what with the constant stream of messages that tell us that our most important relationships are with our cars or deodorants or beer or food or just about anything else, other than ourselves.

I suppose it is habit now, but whenever I start to forget, I think of Sara and her juice.

Sara, my daughter, was about four at the time. I was traveling quite a bit and was gone from home Wednesday though Sunday, two or three weeks a month. Since I arrived home on Sunday night after Sara was asleep, we developed a routine to catch up on each others' lives early Monday mornings. Sara, juice in hand, would awaken me, climb up on the bed and tell me about all the wonderful things that four-year-olds find wonderful, which is almost everything. Now, you're probably thinking that I was inviting trouble by inviting Sara up on the bed with juice in her hand. After all, when you are four, you're not doing your job properly if you don't spill whatever you happen to be holding with some regularity. Hey, I knew that. That's why Sara had just a little juice in a big glass.

Well, after the first few spills it was time for a new plan. That's when Sara got one of those "Tommy-Tippy" cups. You know, the one with the lid, the spout, and the rounded bottom so it would automatically return to the upright position when knocked over, and, most impressively, the guarantee that it could withstand a thermonuclear blast without so much as a drop spilling. That one.

If you have spent any time around truly competent four-year-old children, you know the rest of the story. Of course the spills continued.

If you are asking yourself, "Now, what's the big deal?", I'll tell you. The big deal is I really learned from Sara that how I was feeling about myself dictated how I felt about her. When I was feeling pretty good about myself, the spills were just part of the time we spent together on those Monday mornings; times laughing, talking, being very grown-up and very silly, and learning how to clean up spills. And, when I wasn't feeling so good about myself? "SARA", I would blast, "how many times have I told you...." I still see her scrunched-up face and the big tears welling in her beautiful eyes.

It never had anything to do with four-year-old Sara or with spilling. It really never has to do with anything "out there". It's just about how I feel about me. Am I taking care of my relationship with myself?

But then, you knew that didn't you? I'll bet you'll forget!

Up In Smoke

by Kathleen Carie

There is a saying that we teach what we most need to learn. One of the topics I talk about the most is the value of having strong support people in your life. Now, those who know me know that I am great at telling everybody else what to do, and immensely challenged at all levels of my being when it comes to my letting anyone support me or tell me what I should do.

Ten years ago, I decided that it was time to finally give up smoking. At the time, I was telling all of my friends that I really wanted to find Prince Charming and ride off into the sunset. Jim, a good friend of mine, (and, of course, a strong support person), casually mentioned to me that if I wanted to ride off into the sunset with Prince Charming, having a cigarette dangling out of my mouth was not such an attractive idea. Now honestly, that picture of myself did not bother me as much as his next remark.

"Kathleen," Jim began, "who would want to kiss you? Kissing you would be like licking an ashtray!"

At that moment I had an insight -- maybe this guy has a point here. I momentarily envisioned licking an ashtray and shuddered. "I do believe cigarette smoking is impacting my love life!" (One of the more brilliant insights I have had in my life.)

So I decided, who better to support me than the "jerk" who gave me that fine picture of licking an ashtray? I figured anybody who had the guts to say that to me could, sure as the devil, help me to stop smoking. I called Jim and asked him to support me in becoming a non-smoker. I thought he would be ecstatic that I had actually decided to quit, and that I was asking him to support me. I was in for a rude awakening.

He said to me, "Kathleen, I have heard you say you were going to stop smoking for -- let's see -- how many years have I known you?" The answer, of course, was a whole lot of years. He proceeded to ask, "What's so different this time?" I thought I had him for sure on this one, since I was working on finding a long term relationship, and he had been supporting me to work through a few (okay, a lot!) of intimacy issues. Well, to make a long story even longer, Jim finally responded, "I am unwilling to support you unless you put something on the line to back up your promise."

"What do you mean, put something on the line?" I asked.

Jim answered, "I want you to give me something that I may keep if you break your word and smoke. It has to be something that has so much value to you, that you will be willing to keep your word and not smoke. Because if you break your word, I get to keep whatever you give me."

I thought about it for a moment and said, "No problem. I will give you $500."

Much to my dismay, Jim replied, "No way."

Indignantly, I questioned his response. "What do you mean, no way?"

"Kathleen, I know you would sell your soul to the devil to sneak a cigarette, and happily let me keep the $500."

I was really steamed now! Here was this guy preaching about support -- the very same guy I had just reached out to and asked for support (a big feat in and of itself), and he was turning me down. "What a jerk!" I grumbled to myself, as I lit up another cigarette. "Who needs him? I'll just do it by myself. I'm a mature, sophisticated gal; and furthermore, I was right all along -- support is for babies. Who needs it?" I shrugged as I lit up yet another cigarette.

Several weeks later, I realized I was getting nowhere fast. I called Jim back. Again, he asked me what I was willing to put on the line. We went through about ten ideas. Jim bought none of them. Finally, I blurted out of the blue, "My mom just gave me a gold coin that had belonged to my dad." My dad had just died of cancer.

Jim shouted, "That's it! Give me the gold coin."

My response was immediate and emphatic. "No way! You can't have that -- it means too much to me."

Jim said, "That's the whole point, Kathleen. If it means that much to you, and I have it, then you will think twice before cheating and lighting up."

What steamed my clams even more was that I knew Jim was so cheap (he says frugal), that if I smoked, he would melt the gold coin down and have it made into jewelry for his wife! I knew he would not let me slide and give me back my gold coin if I cheated. And I knew that I could not lie to Jim -- he'd see right through me -- despite the fact that I was a darn good basic story teller.

That was when I began to learn about being committed and keeping an agreement. "Okay, Jim. You win. I will not smoke for thirty days, and you may keep the gold coin for thirty days."

Thirty days passed, and I was bursting at the seams. To tell the truth, the only thing that kept me from not smoking was the fact that my dad's gold coin meant the world to me. In fact, I probably WOULD have sold my soul to the devil for a smoke if it wasn't for the fact that I knew I would never see that gold coin again.

Jim was very proud of me and very excited that I had not smoked for thirty days. I said, "Okay, Jim. I'll be over to get the gold coin tonight."

"Oh, no way!" was Jim's prompt response. "You are on the automatic re-up program."

"So what the hell is the automatic re-up program?" I asked sarcastically.

In his nicest, sweetest voice Jim explained. "It is a program for slimeballs like you, Kathleen, who I know will probably cheat as soon as I give the gold coin back."

Okay. I'll say it. He was right!!! And lucky me, I got to re-up yet one more time. Jim held the gold coin for a total of ninety days.

It has been ten years since I have smoked a cigarette.

Thank you, Jim! Thank you, Dad.

With A Little Help From My Friends

by Joanne Kotjan

Nine years ago this month I got the news. Breast cancer. Malignant. Aggressive. My instinctive reaction was to ask the question: what do I need to do? First I needed to educate myself. What was going on in my body? What were my options? I had to get my affairs in order. I went into surgery immediately, bravely facing that first giant step. Only after the surgery would I find out the scope of my cancer and the treatment plan that best suited me. It was then, as I regained consciousness and started to process the information, that I began to notice the troops that had rallied.

My closest friends brought me love and companionship. Visitors, cards and flowers started arriving in droves. Rarely in my life had I experienced such an outpouring of attention and affection. I had no idea this was just the beginning.

During the next three months of intensive chemotherapy, I was treated to heavy doses of TLC. Needs I didn't know I had, got met in advance of my noticing them. My first chemotherapy session began less than 48 hours after surgery. Visiting hours were over, and the hospital was dark and quiet. I was alone for the first time that day, not knowing what would happen next. A nurse came in, cloaked in metal to protect her from the drugs she was about to administer. I panicked, "What are you going to do to me? Where are you going to put those?" At that moment Janet entered the room. Her timing was impeccable. Just off work from her own healthcare job, she become the spokesperson for my care. After navigating her way through the nurses' station and the logistics of the treatment plan, she stayed with me and helped me to relax and accept my first series of drugs.

Others showed up in equally serendipitous ways. John, knowing I would be spending most of my life in bed, sacrificed his big screen television and had the cable guy install a line in my bedroom. When my hair began to fall out in clumps, he asked if he could have the privilege of shaving my head. Carol took me wig shopping and then whisked me home the minute I ran out of steam. Pat put her life and needs on hold in order to monitor mine. I needed help to shower, to eat, and sometimes even to walk.

I often thought about the notion that "the time to set-up a support network is when you are winning," a reminder that no one is as inclined to create support when it doesn't look like their life is working. In my case, there simply would have been no time.

I was blessed. Not only did I have the benefit of great support, I was part of a loving community that just wouldn't quit. I was never alone in doing everything I could to heal. There were dozens of others, some I never even knew were there, except that I felt the love and kindness that was ever-present in my home. Friends sent prayers as well as flowers. They brought food and food for thought. My healing was truly a group effort, and many of those special names and faces are still with me today.

People do want to help, and are constantly looking for opportunities. Here was a lesson I never would have learned if I'd had the energy to resist. Once I surrendered, I could witness the joy others experience in giving.

Sales: It's the Cat's Meow!

by David Porter

It took me almost 30 years to realize that my life is about sales, and that I am my biggest customer. I regularly buy my own basic stories. But it took a cat to school me on the fine points of salesmanship and enrollment.

I acquired the cat in 1972. Well, truthfully, he acquired me. I was fly fishing on the banks of the Yakima River in eastern Washington. It was a magical place. The smell of sage was intense in the quickening breeze of early evening. I watched intently as my latest offering drifted by—well-placed and inviting. I dismissed the notion that a gallery of bemused trout had gathered a few yards downstream to mock me. As I retrieved the line for yet another cast, I heard behind me a plaintive cry, a cat's meow. A gray feline was poised expectantly on an adjacent boulder. It was more kitten than cat, and seemed a bit worse for wear—a stray, no doubt, cast to the fates by some thoughtless owner. I was not in the mood. This critter had disrupted the tranquillity of the place. I shooed him away and returned to the task at hand.

He was, however, not to be denied; and had worked his way close enough for one final attempt. It was to be a daring sales pitch, a leap of faith. He sprang forth and grabbed my rump with all fours. Yeow! Splat! I landed face down in the river. The trout were surely laughing now.

I was both angry and amused by this development. The cat was still attached, drenched but unflinching. His tenacity and deep amber eyes were compelling. However unreasonable, I was at that moment persuaded of his value. Chester Snatch Bottom, as he came to be called, had successfully enrolled in my family. Thus did my sales training begin. Lesson number one: most sales are made at the emotional level. It is a matter of having the other party see the value you are offering them through their own context. "All right, I will take you home," said I to my little furry friend, "but you must continue to teach me about sales, and about enrollment, and about the value of keeping agreements." He proved to be a good mentor.

During the ensuing nine years Chester did much to establish my faith, confidence, and belief in him. He honored his agreements. He used the litter box, kept the house free of small animals, amused the children and the dog, and engendered much trust and devotion. I also honored my agreements. I fed him well, provided a warm hearth, stroked his chin on a regular basis, and listened to his musings. It was good that I did. He was a wise and perceptive companion. He was also a master salesman. A lingering presence, an alluring purr, a brush of his tail; he did whatever was necessary to secure affection. For those who were too persistent in their attention, he would withdraw just beyond their reach—a strategy sure to increase their ardor. I use this technique myself now with much success.

He was clear about what he wanted and asked directly for it. He participated fully in his own life, and did not have the slightest qualms about enrolling others. Proud of his work, he would often strut about the house with a hapless shrew or mouse in tow. Whatever the family mood—anger or joy, solitude or excitement—he seemed always to make the right moves; to intercede with his affection where it was most needed.

He disappeared one cool morning in early June 1981. There was a frantic search. Neighbors were alerted, posters were hung. I stood an anxious vigil at the back door, anticipating his plaintive cry. None was heard.

Chester never returned.

Had I lost his trust and confidence, or worse, violated some sacred pact? Impossible. Maybe it was not about me at all. Perhaps he had other places to go, other agreements to create, other critters to enroll. I prefer thinking of it that way. I know he is out there—Chester Snatch Bottom, the consummate salesman—and he probably still has the world by the, er, tail.

The Dolphins

by Carol LaCroix

I was about three years old when I almost drowned. My mom and I were visiting friends who had a pool. I remember bobbing up and down at the deep end of the pool while my mother was talking animatedly, clearly enjoying herself, on the patio at the far end. My next memory is of sinking down, deeper and deeper in the water, appreciating the sunny blue sky through the clear water of the pool. Somehow my mom became aware of the trouble I was in, for suddenly I saw her silhouetted against the sky, reaching down to grab hold of my bangs, and pulling me up out of the water. My memory of that particular day ends there.

Fast forward now to 1994, some 40+ years later. By this time in my life I had learned to swim well enough to love the water, even though I hadn't mastered breathing between strokes. My husband and I were in Hawaii on a holiday. It had been "island-paced": slow, easy, extremely un-busy. The day's biggest decision was usually where to eat dinner. Towards the end of our time there we decided to take a snorkeling trip on an ocean raft to some of the nearby islands. I had only snorkeled a few times before and not very successfully. Something about having one airway blocked off and hearing myself inhale and exhale stimulated panic for me—not to mention that snorkeling usually takes place in nice clear water under sunny skies.

On our first stop the ten other snorkelers jumped into their fins and masks, and immediately flopped out of the raft. There was lots of "oohing" and "aahing" and calling to each other, "Did you see the sea turtle?" and "Did you see the ray?", etc., etc. I, on the other hand, was pretty much treading water near the boat trying to get myself horizontal and stay that way. I struggled with my level of expertise in snorkeling—how it should look, how it should feel—for about 45 minutes, then we reboarded to head for another spot on the other side of Lanai. I was feeling pretty sheepish and self-conscious and more than a little like I was missing out on most of the fun.

My focus made a sudden and dramatic shift. Coming directly toward us, about 150 yards ahead, was a school of dolphins—150 or more. As soon as they met our boat they reversed direction, surrounded the raft and began swimming alongside us. It was breathtaking! They leaped and flipped and "conversed" with us (or so we imagined). The babies were especially adorable mimicking the adults. Being in the midst of that energy was more than exciting—it was magical, mystical, inviting.

After a quarter of an hour or so they swam off only to turn back and rejoin us. This time our pilot asked if we wanted to swim with them. Who wouldn't? I didn't have to think about it twice, in fact, I didn't think at all. Completely caught up in the magic of the moment, I slapped on mask and fins and was out of the boat, fully horizontal and totally in control of my breathing and attendant body parts. We were in deep water, quite a distance from the shore, so the water was dark, dark blue and we could only see deeply in the water where shafts of sunlight penetrated. The dolphins were swimming not only all around us but as far down as we could see, in vertical "layers". Human schedules being what they are, we eventually had to reboard and head home.

Not once during that extraordinary experience did I worry about my breathing or have to consciously struggle to swim or stay afloat. Fear fell away in the face of a higher priority—accepting a once-in-a-lifetime invitation to play with the dolphins. With the focus off of me (my image, my memories, my fears), I was 100% present, fully engaged in the activity before me. There was no room for any mental gymnastics because all my energy was focused on participating fully, right here, right now. That was what was most important to me.

I was reminded to accept life's invitations in a most unforgettable way.

Billy Bob Meets The Vet

by Dan Haygeman

Today is the day of dread! It's not taxes or divorce court. It's not a funeral or a friend's farewell. Today I take Billy Bob, our seven month old blue heeler puppy to be 'de-balled'. "He'll be calmer and less aggressive after he's neutered," says a well-meaning friend. Well, hey, who wouldn't be?

His trustingly joyous antics as I lead him toward the vet's glass door do nothing to ease my apprehension at what I'm about to do. I enter the reception area bearing a plastic bag containing several well-chewed toys and his sleeping blanket under one arm and both my hands full of controlling Billy Bob's exuberant entrance. I sign him in and ask that his toenails be trimmed while he's under anesthesia. The receptionist agrees, and comes around the divider to slip a plastic leash and choke collar on Billy and returns his regular collar to me.

Next instant, off she goes, literally dragging poor Billy Bob, my surrogate son, down the tiled hallway. I step over the puddle of urine he left to mark the starting point of his scrambling attempts to get back to me. Hurrying to catch up, I'm faced again by the receptionist, who says, "I can't let you go beyond this door."

"Well, I'd like to make sure you put these toys in with him then," and I hand her the bag. "The towel is what he sleeps on and I'd like him to have it, too." She agrees and drags Billy through the door, letting it close in my face with a whoosh of chemical smells and a reverberation of other dogs barking to challenge the new arrival.

Dazed and saddened, I return to my car and back out of the parking space I had entered only a few minutes before. This wasn't how it was supposed to be. I had wanted to take him back to his kennel and say good-bye myself. It had all happened too fast. At least I could have said, "Stop! I want to get some understanding of what will happen here." After all, Billy had trusted me. And I had trusted the vet.

I spent the next 24 hours being concerned, angry and sad. Practically catatonic from dread, I had let my anxiety run me, rather than taking action before, during or after the 'farewell disaster.' I had no choice now but to trust the process, to hope that everything would be all right, even if it didn't look like the way I wanted it to be.

Billy Bob was characteristically glad to see me when I picked him up from the vet's the next day, his exuberant greeting dulled not the slightest by the huge lampshade-shaped contraption that he would wear for ten days until his stitches were removed. I still marvel at his instant and complete forgiveness of all that had occurred.

It was only ten days later that he let me know that he did, indeed, recall the past upset and discomfort. When we returned to the vet for stitch removal, he caught one whiff of the place and instantly backed away. I knew how he felt. This time, though, I took my time and gently insisted on accompanying him myself for this procedure.

Billy Bob, for his part, seems to love me as totally as ever—whether jumping up on my dress slacks or vigorously demonstrating the calming effect of his neutering by dashing headlong through the house.

Good Intentions

by Arlene Rannelli

I can't believe I'm feeling so frustrated! How could this have happened? This is my good friend, someone I see so much value in! Why doesn't the manager see what I see?

These were some of the questions I asked myself when the local manager fired a friend of mine, a friend I held in high esteem. I was angry and upset. I was worried for my friend. Most of all, I wanted nothing to do with the manager who acted, in my mind, so out of integrity, so blind to the truth, so ... cruel.

The more I went over this in my mind, the more depressed I began to feel. I knew I was scheduled to be back in the office the following week, and I was dreading it. How could it be anything but a terrible experience, given the way I was feeling?

I called my area manager to see if we could reschedule, or send someone else. This was not possible. I didn't see how I would be the least bit effective. My area manager suggested I bracket my feelings and do the best job I could.

After our conversation, I felt like I was back to square one. I didn't like, or agree with what had happened nor how it had been handled. The local manager didn't seem to think that how I felt about it was very important. I did not understand this and started to feel resentful toward the manager for a growing list of reasons.

Then I asked myself what I wanted out of this situation. I began to remember why I worked for this company in the first place. I brought to mind the role I believe I play in the lives of the people I come in contact with. I noticed I began to feel better. I recalled other times in my relationship with this local manager when we did not see eye to eye, and that this was not something new in our relationship. More importantly, we had both survived countless disagreements and we were both still here, doing what was important to us, doing whatever it took to make things work, and to make it the best that we knew how. I let go of my negative judgments, and instead, chose to focus on the fact that we did, indeed, have a mutual goal. It is my opinion that anyone who works for this company has to have some underlying good intentions for whatever they do—even if, at times, I don't understand what they are.

By the time I returned to the office the following week, I was fine. I had worked it through my mind in such a way that I no longer felt any negative emotions towards the person who had fired my friend; and as a matter of fact, we got along better than we had for a very long time.

The belief that "everyone has a good intention somewhere inside of him or her" has seen me through a lot in life. It is the way I choose to keep moving forward.

Scared Spitless

by Jim Sorensen

I'd always been terrified of public speaking. I had a severe speech impediment as a small child. But with much thanks to a very skillful and compassionate speech therapist, I was taught to "keep Sammy snake in his cage" (my tongue behind my teeth), and I learned to speak clearly by the time I was eight. The problem was, I was left with the fear of being ridiculed and teased, a fear I built on with every possible situation, real or imagined.

This would have been all fine and good. A person can lead a very happy and fulfilled life and never speak in public. But, here's where the problem occurred. I took a sales position with a new company and part of the job description was group sales presentations. I panicked. I wanted the position. I really wanted to work for this company. Just without this public speaking thing.

My first step toward solution was to visit a Toastmasters club. I did a one minute talk. I was quite the natural. I received an amazing amount of sympathy, advice and the "um" award. I even had one kind-hearted gentleman tell me that public speaking may not be for everyone.

I then decided it would just work out naturally. Deep denial. I was scheduled for my first presentation. I was scared spitless. I got up hoping for a miracle. I shook and babbled throughout the entire presentation. Someone in the second row even told me he could hear the change in my pockets! Told me that during my presentation. No miracle.

The second time, shored up by some very strong support, I spoke again. This time my internal mantra was "Don't be nervous, Don't be nervous". Same result.

Afterwards I was whining and recounting my disastrous experience, when a very wise person overheard my dilemma. She told me my problem was that in repeating "don't be nervous," I was affirming a negative. What I should be doing is affirming the positive. I should be saying to myself, "Be calm, Be calm."

I was so excited! I knew this would work. The next time I got up at the front of the room, I chanted "Be calm, Be calm". All of a sudden a voice deep inside me said, "B.S.! Look at you, you're shaking all over!" Back to the drawing board.

I went home alone and defeated, loaded down with embarrassment and feedback. I woke up in the middle of the night during a very restless sleep, and was struck by a thought. "I'm a nervous person. I may always be a nervous person. So given that, what can I do to be effective in these presentations?" I'd decided to embrace reality. What a novel concept.

So the next time I got up to speak, I was prepared. After shaking and babbling for my allotted time, I closed my presentation with, "You must know this is a good product, or I wouldn't have been willing to put myself through what you just saw me put myself through." I had one of the most successful sales events in the company's history. Reality had worked.

As the months went by I used my nervousness to add humor and energy to my presentations. And then one magical day I was on stage and a strange thing happened. I could talk and think at the same time. How wonderful. I'd learned a very valuable lesson: Tell the truth, especially to myself.

Seeing With My Heart

by Gerri Moulton

When I was eight years old, I decided that I was an artist. I had painted my first (and only) picture with oils. It was a mountain range reflected in water, all purple and snowcapped, on a board about the size of a postcard. That was the size of the picture I copied from. I was encouraged to do this by my godfather, Uncle Dick, and he praised me when I finished. But I was teased unmercifully by the rest of my family, and so I kept the picture to myself and looked at it only when I was alone. I promised myself that someday I would run away to those mountains.

Some years later during geography lessons, I once more saw those mountains. It was British Columbia, and there were not only mountains but the ocean as well. Although we lived in Montreal, Quebec, I began to think that I must have lived there at some time. I begged my mother to tell me if I was really adopted. That was the beginning of years of daydreaming in which I fantasized about marrying a Mountie, or becoming a movie star, anything that would take me away to the ocean and my mountains.

I never did anything about those fantasies for fear of being laughed at and criticized. There never was enough money to go traveling. Eventually I stopped daydreaming and got on with my everyday life.

During my early working years I had a job with a railway company. After a year on the job I was entitled to a free trip up to 1500 miles. I was thrilled! However, the farthest I got was Winnipeg, in the very flat prairies. I didn't even manage to find a Mountie there.

The longing never really left, but there was always something or someone to keep me where I was: a job, boyfriend, husband, children etc. Then, early in 1980, I had an opportunity to accompany my mother to Vancouver, British Columbia to visit my grandfather. One can only imagine the excitement I felt! I was not only going to see those beautiful mountains, but I would actually be at The Pacific Ocean. I spent the first few days walking around the seawall in the rain, and felt a sense of peace and calm like never before. I belonged here. After five days of intense fog and rain, the skies cleared, the sun came out and there they were—my mountains—just as they were in my painting. The most beautiful mountains I have ever seen.

I decided that somehow I would do whatever was necessary to get back, and I did. That Thanksgiving Day my husband and I arrived in Vancouver in a rusty station wagon with a trailer full of our possessions, and enough money to live frugally for about a month. We quickly found work and an apartment very close to the mountains and water. I was home.

About a year later I heard about the concept of "holding the vision," and I knew that's what I had been doing since I was eight years old. Even though my picture wasn't always in my mind, it was in my heart. And now my heart is home.

Raising A Magical Child

by Brenda Sorensen

Imagination is the magic of childhood, and children are full of magic. It's one of the many gifts of having a child that I have come to cherish most as a mother. My daughter Katelyn never ceases to amaze me and reminds me constantly what life, love and self-expression are all about.

Children left to their own devices have an amazing amount of creativity. Often, Katelyn will suggest "let's pretend that the carpet is the water, the couch or the bed is the boat." She will enthusiastically exclaim, "I know, I know, let's pretend this..., or let's do that..." It's so easy in one brief second to squash that energy and enthusiasm with a "not now, I'm busy," or "I'm tired," or worse yet, "that can't really happen." But I've learned to allow (and enjoy!) her creative expression however it shows up.

I remember a time when our daughter was 3 $\frac{1}{2}$ years old and she and my husband were going to the video store. She came out of her bedroom ready to go, dressed in a pink and yellow flowered party dress, black socks pulled up midway to her calves, pink and purple multi-colored tennis shoes, her long hair sticking out of her ponytail every which way, and topped it all off with a jeans jacket. She proudly looked up at her dad and said, "I put black socks on so that I would match your black shirt." My "adult" fashion critic was not singing silent praises, in fact, I was actually counting my blessings that

I was not going along. Fortunately, I recognized that it is this same "adult" critic that has squashed so much of my own creativity; so instead I hugged her and praised her for getting herself all ready to go and told her she looked great.

Another time she was painting with tempura paints. We couldn't find her paint shirt so she was painting without a shirt on at all. I went out of the room for a few minutes and when I came back in, she had already started painting her arms and tummy! Instead of yelling or getting upset, her dad and I carried her outside with her paint and grabbed the camera. We all giggled and laughed and then carried her into the bathtub to clean her up. It's a great memory we can all look back on.

Children need to be encouraged, and those moments of expression nurtured. It might take a little extra energy, a bit more time, some letting go of our own old beliefs about what's "proper" or "prudent", but the payoffs are great.

Children Are Natural Winners

by Jeff Gaines

A friend of mine told me a story that wonderfully captures the essence of creating agreements. He was sitting peacefully in his living room when his three-year-old daughter ran up to him excitedly and said "Daddy, come with me!" and started pulling him where she wanted him to go. He said, "No, honey, I don't want to go right now." She persisted, and he knew from experience that she would pull at him until he yielded or she collapsed from exhaustion. Deciding that the latter of these two choices might border on child abuse, he said, "Sit down and let me explain something."

He sat her down and told her, "If you want something from me, you have to give me something that I want." She looked at him somewhat confused. He continued, "Now, if you were to give me a big kiss and a hug, I'd be more willing to come with you." She paused, then asked, "Daddy, will you come with me?" He answered, "What will you give me?" She replied tentatively, "A kiss?" "And a hug," he answered. She nodded excitedly and started off toward her destination. "What about my kiss and hug?" he reminded her gently. She ran back to him, pecked him on the cheek, and patted his shoulders in what can only be described as a drive-by hugging, then ran off again. Deciding he had made his point, he strode proudly across the room after her.

Now, some people would look at this story and see it as bribery or manipulation. I see a great example of win/win agreement creation. Children seem to get the concept of win/win much more quickly than we mature and advanced adults. I think it's because of two things: to play win/win, I have to know what winning is to me, and I have to be winning in my own life. If I'm not winning, it's very hard for me to want you to win. Children may not be able to clearly articulate exactly what winning is to them, but they are very clear about what they want, and pursue it with reckless abandon! They haven't yet learned that being responsible, at least in the eyes of the world at large, means not getting what they want.

Children seem to have a rich full experience of life much more easily than most adults. I think the reason is simple. Kids think, "What do I want?" and then set out to get it, holding nothing back. Adults think, "What can I have?" and then learn how to cope with that. I see this story as another example of how much I have to learn from children.

Tradition

by Elisabeth Revell

Christmas is a big deal around my parents' house. They have many rituals that have been in place from before I was born. Who knows how or why many of them started?

Each year Dad and I were in charge of the tree lights and Mom, the ornaments. While we were working on the lights, Mom would put on Gene Autry's Christmas Album (the first one we listened to each year), break open the first carton of eggnog and take pictures.

Part of the ritual when we took down the tree the prior year was to unscrew the bulbs from the strings of colored lights and store them in a box. We would carefully wind up the wires and store them separately. Then, the following year, we would reinsert the bulbs. I was the bulb inserter and tester. I remember how much I enjoyed watching each bulb light. There are many photographs of me holding one bulb up to each cheek and smiling.

Dad was very meticulous about the placement of the lights. He would start at the top of the tree with a single clear bulb to show off the angel and work his way down, laying lights from the trunk of the tree to the tip of each branch and back again, making sure the wires were hidden. I would race to complete strands of carefully selected bulbs (no two of the same color next to each other) and test them in time for Dad. Dad was slow, but it took quite a while to screw in all those bulbs. We had tall trees, thus many strands of lights, and I would get a little slow by the time we got halfway through the tree. Every once in a while Mom would tell Dad he missed a spot.

Each year we did this ritual.

One year, when I was in high school, I asked my father why we removed the bulbs and reinserted them each year. He considered it and said it was so we knew each bulb was good. I told him we could determine that by just plugging in the whole string. We decided there wasn't any valid reason, other than that we had always done it this way, then we started laughing.

Change happened quickly after this discovery. After leaving the bulbs in their sockets for a couple of years, we moved onto little white lights. Dad discovered that if he randomly laid the strings on the branches it looked just as beautiful. This year he almost threw the strings on the tree (although Mom still alerted him to spots he missed).

Just because it's the way we've always done it doesn't necessarily make it the best way.

The Lion's Den

by David Porter

Children are a gift. I have three of them, all boys. What they are here to learn seems less important than what they are here to teach, especially to me. The teacher will appear when the student is ready to learn. I hope always to be ready.

I grew up in Richmond, Virginia. From age eight until my early twenties, I lived in a sprawling colonial style house on a hillside. At one end of the house was my father's study. It was furnished with a large flat-top wooden desk. A generous easy chair with matching ottoman in burgundy leather occupied the space in front of a wood burning fireplace. There were shelves overflowing with textbooks and medical journals. He was a distinguished physician and teacher.

My father spent a lot of time in his study—in the house but not at home. No doubt, he was busy with medical school affairs and patient care issues. I entered this room cautiously and then only with the intent of purposeful communications. He was never rude or unresponsive but somehow seemed inaccessible. Perhaps he learned this from his father, a distinguished theologian, and a stern, formal man who always addressed his wife as Mrs. Porter.

Today I live in a sprawling house on a hillside in Everett, Washington. I have a study with a large flat-top oak desk, a high back burgundy leather chair, and a wood burning fireplace. Floor-to-ceiling bookshelves grace one end of the room. Glass-paned French doors separate my study from the adjacent kitchen. This makes it easy for me to keep track of family comings and goings. Good fathers always do.

I spend a lot of time in my study. Naturally there are bills to pay, investments to manage, programs to prepare, and myriad telephone calls to return. It is necessary and appropriate that I be concerned with such things. I, too, want to distinguish myself. It is the way of the Porters.

Of course, my children are always welcome to join me in the study. It wasn't long ago that my oldest son, Matthew, came to the doorway and said, "Dad, I would like to talk with you. Is now a good time?" I was poised behind my desk, no doubt concerned with some important "affairs of state". I leaned back and in my most fatherly tone responded, "Sure, Matt, what's on your mind?" I motioned him to the high back chair. He paused and said, "Actually I prefer to talk to my real dad, not the one sitting behind the desk."

Although his comment was made without malice, it had a sting that I still feel today. My cherished beliefs about being a great parent and father were shaken to the core. I do not remember details of the ensuing discussion. I do remember that in that moment I realized what he was here to teach me. It was about being fully present with others—about creating safety and being accessible. I cannot think of anything more important to do as a parent, or as a human, for that matter.

We Porters have to get a grip. There are lots of ways for me to distinguish myself. I just don't want to wait so long to find out about them.

Asking the Right Questions

by Arlene Rannelli

Have you ever wondered how to change something that you don't like? How to determine why whatever is not working—is not working? How to get what you really want out of life?

My daughter was 13 and I had no idea what to do about our relationship. We were arguing a lot—about cleaning up the house, what time to come home at night, which places were appropriate for her to go and which were not—your typical topics for teenagers at home, I'm told. Yet I found myself feeling hurt and rejected, resistant, and determined to be right about whatever point we were discussing. I was frustrated. I resented her for not being the daughter I thought she should be. I felt guilty over some of my choices in life, choices that brought me to this moment, as a single, workaholic Mom with a determined, sometimes seemingly uncontrollable child. I WAS STUCK BIG TIME.

One day my daughter informed me that she'd had enough, too. She wanted to go live with her dad for the summer. I felt as though my heart had just been ripped from my body! Now how was I ever going to build a healthy relationship with my daughter?

It turned out that I was asking the wrong question. It was hard for me to accept, especially after 13 years of being a mother-in-training, that in order to create that healthy relationship with my daughter, I needed first a healthy relationship with myself. My first thought was,

"Don't I have enough on my plate already—what with my demanding job and my equally demanding daughter? From diapers to diplomas, aren't I supposed to be focusing on her? Doesn't taking time out for me mean that I am selfish and self-absorbed?

Well, to answer a question with a question, who knows better than me what I want out of life? Only I know what is most important to me. Only I can do the work entailed in determining my purpose in life. Finding the meaning, the purpose in my life was the most powerful experience I had ever had! I learned what was most important to me. I made the commitment to myself to live in that purpose. My daughter moved back in with me that September and we have never looked back. Our relationship is terrific.

I've heard it said that "You can be right, or you can have what you want." Having what I want is often easier when I ask myself the right questions.

Laughter is the Best Medicine

by Diane Kennedy

I occasionally conduct humor workshops. When I was first getting started understanding humor and its place in our lives, I read Norman Cousins' experiences with the healing power of laughter during his illness. I discovered that when we laugh, our body releases endorphins that are natural painkillers, very much like morphine. They are very powerful. Laughter, therefore, is very therapeutic. Laughter changes our physiology, it changes our chemistry. I was very excited about this discovery.

A friend and I attended a humor conference some ways from home, and on the way back we stopped for a little "retail therapy." I picked up a pair of children's glasses, the kind with the eyeballs already painted on, and when I put them on, my friend and I went into hysterics. I looked at myself in the mirror with these silly glasses on. It changed the whole reality of how I looked, and who I was, and I couldn't help but laugh.

These glasses became my first aid kit for laughter. Whenever I was upset, or feeling down, or something was not going well, I would put on these glasses and break up. They created an instantaneous different world. A silly world.

The next time my parents came to visit, I told them I had just had my eyes tested, and that I wanted to show them my new glasses. Then I left the room. When I returned, I had these silly glasses on. My parents were used the seeing their daughter a certain way. They had 35 years of experience in seeing me that way. My appearance at my entrance defied those expectations. My father, my mother, my brother and I began to laugh until we cried.

Everybody wanted to try on those glasses. Now Mom was a very conservative person. Very proper. She never told a joke in her life, never said anything in jest, never swore or was unladylike in any way. But when she put on those silly glasses, the two of us laughed so hard we were afraid we were going to wet our pants. We raced each other to the bathroom. As I was younger and more agile, I got in there first. Seconds later I heard Mom outside the door, still overwhelmed with laughter. Then there was a splash. I didn't have to guess what that meant.

This became one of our family's favorite stories. I gave Mom a pair of these silly glasses to take home with her. She tried them on for her friends, and called to tell me that none of her friends liked those glasses. I replied, "Well, Mom, do you like those glasses? Do they make you laugh? Then that's all that counts. Because when you are laughing, you're the one who is getting all the benefits."

I often shared this family story with the people at my workshops. A few years later I had the honor of sharing it with family and friends at my mother's funeral, after she had died of lung cancer. We laughed and we cried together, just as my mom and I had done. The value of sharing this funny family moment was in renewing our bond, and bringing to life a person and a time that was special to us. Laughter brings us back, again and again, to our humanity, to the moments and people and emotions that we treasure. I know when I put on those glasses, even to this day, Mom and I are sharing the laughter and love we knew then.

Dry Rot

by Jim Sorensen

The hardest direction for a human to look in, with any degree of clarity, is at the self. Many of us could assess our close friends, our co-workers, our mate or spouse very quickly and do it with a great deal of comfort. But when it comes to making a clear assessment of one's self, it becomes quite uncomfortable. If I don't know there is a problem and don't do anything about it, somehow that feels better than if I do know there is a problem and don't do anything about it.

My wife and I remodeled our home when our daughter was a little over a year old. This was the first major remodel I'd ever done. We hired a contractor. One of the first things I said to him was, "What is everything that an unskilled laborer can do?" Because I am cheap—and extremely unskilled.

One of his suggestions was to remove all the old vinyl from the kitchen floor to check for dry rot or carpenter ants (both are very popular items here in the Northwest). He warned that it would be difficult to find a house over fifteen years old that didn't have one or both. I panicked. What if we took up the vinyl and found one of those huge subterranean rot caverns into which unsuspecting homeowners are required by law to pour all their money? I clearly didn't want any part of that. I came up with a brilliant plan to put a new layer of vinyl over the top and instruct everyone that enters our house to walk more softly from now on.

But thanks to a very convincing wife that came from the "If you're going to do something, do it right!" School of Home Repair, I took on the job. I took my trusty putty knife and I began scraping away the old vinyl. And scraping. And scraping. And I found not only two layers of relatively new vinyl laid down by past procrastinators, but underneath those was an old linoleum floor with a tar base! Quite a joy to remove. I kept scraping. It was about two o'clock in the morning and I'd vowed for about the hundredth time not to do another remodeling project for the rest of my life, when all of a sudden the putty knife, my hand, and the rest of my arm slipped through the floor! I had found dry rot. (Not to mention a very large colony of carpenter ants!)

I don't remember joy being one of my internal experiences upon the discovery. I wasn't even in the joy neighborhood. I woke up my wife in order to share with her my lack of joy in the situation. I was not pleased.

But I am quite pleased now. I took the risk, and I did the work. With a little courage, a little excavation, some new materials and some old-fashioned hard work, I know I have a very solid foundation in that kitchen. I know what's under there.

When most of us hit an area where there may be work, we tend to procrastinate. The procrastinating mind says, "If I put it off, it will get better on its own. Usually, though, it doesn't tend to work this way, even though I think it might, this time. What are the chances that, amidst all that dry rot and infestation, the carpenter ants down there are saying, "Hey, we've done all we can here. Let's pack up and go to the neighbors!" Not high.

Just as there was dry rot in my home, I had a bit of dry rot in my life. There were some worn places, some fragile places in my life where I suspected there might be a problem, and I was hoping that without my attention, the mess would clean itself up and move on. So with a metaphorical putty knife in hand, I went to work on my life just as I had done on the kitchen floor. I went to work before the problems got worse, before I would have to pay a much higher price to resolve them.

Now, not only do I have a really solid foundation in that kitchen, but more importantly, I have a very solid foundation where it really counts ... in my life.

The Learning Curve

by Pam Mason

It was 6:15 in the morning, and I was in a hurry. I was getting ready to drive to work and had asked my husband, Richard, to gather his dry cleaning together so I could drop it off at the cleaner's on my way. I was fearful of being late to work, which would mean that I would have several impatient high school students lined-up outside of my classroom door, with a cacophony of blame sounding my way when I got there.

"Where are your clothes?" I screamed shrilly up the stairs. Silence. "Richard, you are making me late! I hate waiting for you. Get down here with your clothes!" Nothing.

As I'm poised at the bottom of the stairs, hands on hips, ready to yell again, a huge armload of clothes comes flying down at me, as hard as Richard could throw them. I'm covered with jackets, pants and ties. I am enraged. How dare he?

I gather up the clothes, take them to the car and stuff them in the trunk, hoping there's a patch of oil in there somewhere that will leave a stain that will never come out. I drive to work, fuming all the way. I pass the dry cleaner and give it the one finger salute, muttering, "Those clothes can rot in my trunk for all I care. He'll never see them again!"

I'm on time for work, but my students are still cross with me. I quickly show them what cross really looks like. They're no match for me. First period gets a pop quiz I'd been saving up for just such an occasion. My head is beginning to ache. Second period gets a pressure essay to write in 55 minutes. I'm showing them who's boss! My headache has turned into a migraine. The next hour is my preparation time and my classroom is empty. I put my head down on my desk and cry.

All I really wanted to do was get the dry cleaning done, and get to work on time. Somewhere along the line I had completely lost track of my original purpose. Now I had a choice: I could beat myself up for getting off track and having a really cranky morning, or I could begin to course correct. I see I still have 25 minutes left in my prep period. The dry cleaner is only five minutes away ....

Retrieving Richard's clothes from the trunk, I deliver them to the counter with an extra flourish. I ask, "Do you have pick-up and delivery service?" They do! My headache dissipates and I get back to work in enough time to cross a whole category off my to-do list. I am ecstatic! I now have a designated driver for our dirty clothes, and a workable way to get the dry cleaning done. Success is mine!

Whose Problem Is It, Anyway?

by Brent Stewart

Even-tempered, and proud of it. That's me. I grew up in a family where we didn't display our feelings very much, and I quickly learned how to conceal mine. As an adult I went into the business world and found that my ability to display little emotion was a tremendous asset. Nothing would upset me. But what worked in the business world didn't seem to be nearly as effective in my relationships with women. Somehow, in spite of my 'even temperament', my relationships with women didn't seem to work out. I couldn't understand why women were so emotional. It seemed to me they had some kind of 'problem'.

It all came to a head when I met *her*. She was fiery, out there, open and demanding. I was reserved, private, closed and easy-going. I guess you could call it an attraction of opposites. True, we produced a lot of chemistry, but at the heart of the matter, we really didn't understand each other.

The first time she got angry, really angry, I practically went into shock. I wasn't used to seeing that kind of anger, except on the movie of the week! I felt uncomfortable and helpless, like a small boat in a hurricane. Rather than deal with the issue, which seemed minor to me, I began to withdraw and make judgments. I waited for the waves to subside. It was going to be a long wait. As the relationship unfolded we began to show our dissatisfaction with each other. She sometimes referred to me as "Mr. Spock." I took it as a compliment.

Her problem was that she wasn't enough like Spock to suit me. *She* was overemotional. *She* had no self-control. I began to hide things from her that I thought she might find upsetting, in order to avoid "setting *her* off." She sensed this and began to distrust me. There were many wonderful things in the relationship, but there was no papering over this issue. I was overwhelmed by her range and she was emotionally starved by mine. It was clear we were both ready to call it quits.

However, we did something I'd never done before. We decided to get some counseling. I'd never been to a counselor before because I thought that counselors were for dysfunctional people, and as anybody could tell you, I thought I was extremely functional. I did end up agreeing to go, because, after all, *she* did have this problem.

Funny thing was, the counselor gave us exercises that had to do with expressing our feelings. I hated the exercises. Furthermore, I found them to be extremely difficult. While I was hopelessly stuck, my partner could do the exercises with ease. Gradually a new idea began to filter through me. Maybe *I* was the one who had the work to do. Maybe *I* was disconnected from my feelings and the reason I had such an issue with her was because *I* was so out of touch with myself! Somewhere inside a light was dawning. Perhaps her problem was really *my* problem.

We still parted company, but with a difference. I didn't go away with the illusion that we'd broken up because of her issues. I went away with the knowledge that I had work to do. Had it not been for this insight I would have simply moved on to a new relationship and found, to my surprise: another woman with the same issue as the last one!

Thanks to this shift, my new relationship is growing rather than shrinking. And, thanks to some patient women, I'm coming to understand that a healthy relationship starts with me.

A Bold Step

by Catherine Elliott

I loved the way he looked at me when I pushed him against the plate-glass window and kissed him for the first time. I was thrilled that diners at "Portland's most romantic restaurant" turned to look at us. I loved my bravery. In that luscious moment, I met every need I ever had. I was alive.

But I couldn't keep this up.

I was good at romance and seduction. I wasn't so good at staying in a relationship. And if I did stay, I wasn't good at staying passionate. So when that man wanted a deeper, more committed relationship, I got scared. Over the next year, I acted like I was in a Woody Allen movie with tortured good-bye scenes. We parted. I heard he married the next year.

Eventually, I wanted something beyond that first thrill. Then it occurred to me: I didn't have a clue what to do next! I was a pro in taking the first steps in a relationship and had become more familiar than I wanted to be with the last steps, but I had no real idea how to develop a committed relationship.

So, I got to work—reluctantly at first, since it seemed so foreign. I started learning that relationships that work, take work; and that the quality of a relationship is my job. (This was hard for me to face.) I also realized I didn't have a very good support network for this new venture, as most of my friends tended to have short-term relationships too. I kept them as friends, but I also began to befriend people who were in long-term relationships. I asked them questions like: "Do you still feel excited like you did when you first met?" [Not quite -- it's a different, deeper excitement]; "Are you ever bored in your relationship?" [Yes]; and "Do you ever feel like flirting with anyone else?" [Sometimes, but I'm glad to be with ____].

I eventually proposed to a dear friend, who took a year to consider whether I really meant it. And now, we're newly married! I may not always feel like I did when I pushed my old love up against the plate-glass window, but I am very grateful to be here with my husband, lying together at the end of the day.

I know I'll be learning about relationships for the rest of my life. And, who knows, one day I may just get the urge to show my husband all I've learned in a most outrageous and public way!

My Romance

by Carol Peringer

I'm the kind of girl who likes a little romance in life. Not too much, mind you, but I do enjoy a little "hearts and flowers" kind of stuff now and then. My future husband was an artist, and I assumed that art and romance would go hand in hand. Besides, I was heavily in lust and infatuation, and everything he did seemed romantic to me. He could put gas in my car and I'd rave to all my friends about what a prince he was.

Well, you know what they say about the word assume! After we'd been married for a year or so, I started to notice that there really wasn't much going on in the romance department. No romantic dinners alone, no flowers or surprise gifts. It began to dawn on me that he'd never been much of a romantic at all. So I sat him down and explained to him how important romance is to me, and could he please do more romantic stuff? He asked me to make him a list. A list! I tried to explain to him that lists don't exactly cause me to swoon, and if I have to spell it out for him in advance, that ain't my concept of romance!

Now I spent the next couple of years in a very attractive, charming and alluring way bitching and whining at him to be more romantic. Guess what? It didn't exactly produce the result I was looking for. Somewhere along the way I began to realize that my husband is not a romantic. I also began to remember that love is about joyfully accepting people (even husbands) just the way they are, without requiring them or expecting them to be different than how they are. I must admit that actually getting to a place of acceptance about this didn't happen overnight. It was hard to let go of that fundamental fact of life taught to me in my youth by none other than Walt Disney....'It's the man's job to be romantic"!! I spent some time grieving because Walt misled me, but eventually I turned the page.

If it's to be, it's up to me. Since I'm the person in my marriage who loves romance, I decided I'd better get busy! So I started preparing fancy meals, sending the kids to the sitters and greeting him at the door in saran wrap. I planned the vacations for two and started buying him gifts for no reason at all. Believe me, he always participated in these events and loved it.

I no longer expect him to become a romantic fool, in fact, I'm pretty sure that's not going to happen. He does appreciate what I do and how important it is to me. I'm having more fun, and more romance. And every once in a while, he gives me a surprise that really knocks me off my feet: one year, on my birthday, he sent flowers to my mother with a note that said, "Thank you for giving birth to the woman that I love." Now if that isn't romantic, I don't know what is!

A Hot Time in the Hot Tub Tonight

by Brent Stewart

I always thought it would be great to own a hot tub. Those brochures of sexy-looking couples cuddling and leering at the camera were quite, uh, inspirational. Even better than visions of sugar plums dancing in my head were visions of bubbly jet massages, frothy foam parties, and best of all, a romantically lit playpen. These visions had "delicious decadence" written all over them. Hot tubs spelled hot times for me. Needless to say, I eventually ordered one; and when the tub finally arrived, I couldn't wait to get started.

Well, the hot tub has been an enormous success, but not in any of the ways I initially imagined. In spite of all the fancy water nozzles, we rarely turn the jets on; preferring the silence of the night to the commotion of the bubble machinery. We don't turn on the romantic underwater lighting, either. The darkness of the night sky sprinkled with starlight makes a far more romantic backdrop. And parties? Only two in the last two years. And, as far as sex goes, we discovered that a hot tub is not a particularly great place to have sex after all. (Okay, maybe it is ONCE.)

Many exotic places are memorable once—for example, airline washrooms (so I'm told). After the first time, the novelty goes downhill fast. I wonder, after trying the airline washroom, do people go home and regularly use the broom closet? But, I digress. The point is, nowadays if we're feeling amorous, we go back into the house.

What is the hot tub good for, then? In spite of being a flop in the Guinness Book of Records for Sex, the tub has benefited our relationship in ways I never imagined. At the end of nearly every day we go for a soak and a talk. Snug in the tub, we have great conversations— conversations we probably would never have sitting in the living room. We clear anything that we need to sort out between us; any upset feelings, resentments or unresolved conflicts. We bring up any difficulties from the day we need to let go of before we sleep. We mention something we've learned from the day. Finally, we acknowledge ourselves, each other, and occasionally other people for things we appreciate. The result is we go to sleep each night "clear" with each other and with the day.

People used to tell me that intimacy was more important than sex. I didn't believe it. If you don't believe it either, buy a hot tub!

When Love Goes Down The Drain

by Leigh Farrell

I always chuckle if I see a hair in a bathtub.

When my husband and I were first married, our bathtub was always full of his thick brown hair after he took his morning shower. He loved to vigorously rub his head with a towel, not only because it felt invigorating, but being an efficient, practical and busy man (he is an energizer rabbit!) it meant less time using a hair dryer.

He had an abundance of hair—enough to fill the state of Rhode Island—and he left equally abundant amounts of it behind in the tub. When my turn came to step into the tub, the hair on the bottom drove me crazy. It felt dirty, intrusive, thoughtless; and besides, it clogged the drain. Months of this revolting behavior finally brought things to a head (so to speak).

This insensitive Martian (men are from Mars, you know) had to be taught respectable bathroom etiquette. We had a family meeting. I whined. He listened. I was armed with facts and feelings and the support of my female friends who thought it was gross and disgusting. (Ah, Ha! I was right!) He agreed. He promised to change. I was ecstatic. I could step into a clean, shiny, white ceramic wonder. I was in heaven.

And then the hair slowly began creeping back into the tub. First erratically, then more steadily, and finally, consistently. I nagged. It stopped ... temporarily. I was convinced he wasn't trying. If he really loved me, he'd remember. Normally, he's such a reasonable and sensitive man. Was there a Freudian interpretation here? Was our relationship clogged? Going down the drain? I nagged again. He repented sincerely, but gradually the hair crept back in. I resented it. And him. And soon, by implication, all insensitive men!

Sanity was restored once I realized that intimacy and closeness and fun were more important in our relationship than no hair in the bathtub. I saw it clearly as my issue, since I knew that he could be knee-deep in hair and still not notice! By nagging and wanting to be right about the "yukiness" of the hair in the bathtub, I was sabotaging the very intimacy that was truly most important to me. So I changed my point of view to be in line with my priorities. He was ecstatic.

Now when I see hair in the bathtub, I just smile.

Back In the Swim of Things

by Kate Menard

I am into convenience in a big way. Like recently I purchased a pair of loafers so I wouldn't have to waste time tying my shoes! So it was rather a challenge for me to find a way of becoming more physically fit within the context I held around exercise.

I had been of the opinion that exercise is, at best, a chore. Especially if I actually have to go somewhere to have this experience. I like my life to be as uncomplicated as a Seven - Eleven. Since I am impulsive and spontaneous by nature, I must save all my sense of structure for use at the office. Outside the office, anything that takes more than 30 seconds to set-up is not a priority. And, I'm a little short on the big city survival tactics I need just to ride a bike here in Toronto. So I scrapped the "load the bike on the roof and drive to the park so I can unload the bike and ride around the park so I can re-load the bike so I can take it home" idea and went for a simpler mode of transportation: walking the dog.

My huge husky used to pull me around the block. Now, at eight and a half years of age, if I stop, she stops. I can beat her home. It's not so much of a walk as it is a meander, an amble, a stroll.

On with my search. Next I tried the health club, a sort of Love Connection for people in perfectly matched tights and togs. Mel Gibson meets Elle MacPherson. However, I do not have a perfect body, or matching anything, and I don't do stuff that hurts! Only half of the health club clientele seemed to really enjoy exercising, the other 50% seemed to have a frozen smile pasted on their faces, as if to say, "Any moment now I know the enjoyment will come." One look at my own sweaty body, red puffy face, and limp, stringy hair and I knew: this was not a pretty sight! Time to move on.

Then, joy of joys, I had an insight. I remembered a great love from my childhood—swimming! I recalled summer days that flew by as I splashed and stroked my way along the St. Lawrence River. It was so much fun then that I decided to give it another try. I found a nice, egalitarian community center, where fashion is not the focus. I can spend time on my own (after all, I am much less available for demands when completely submerged in H_2O); and best of all, even if I am sweating, nobody notices it! I come out of the pool feeling refreshed and cool. Even though I don't like exercise, swimming is fun!

The Devil's in the Details

by Jeff Gaines

Completion. Attention to details. Dotting the i's and crossing the t's. These expressions are, for some of us, like the sound of fingernails on a chalkboard; it ranks right up there with "taxes" and "'till death do us part." I have always fancied that detail-oriented people must be hyper-driven, nuclear intelligent, hard-working people. Yet recently, a mentor of mine, a man I seriously respect and admire for his extremely anal tendencies, told me that he is the laziest person he knows. I was convinced he was just being modest, kidding, or flat-out lying. Because we all know that it's the nose to the grindstone, sleeves rolled-up, sleeps at the office type of hard-working guy with the blinders on that gets it all handled, right? And the rest of us, well—the fewer details the better. Or so I thought.

One of the many lives I lead is that of a service manager for a computer networking company. As a high tech company, we frequently experience periods of calm followed by periods of intense craziness. I had resigned myself to believe that this just goes with the territory. But the closer I examined the pattern, the more I realized I had been creating it! In fact, I could identify the pattern in every area of my life. Damn. Once again I found myself the source of my biggest frustrations.

The pattern looks like this: Things are going smoothly. I feel clear about where I am and where I am going. I track, I monitor, I maintain. Then this gets a little boring. I find myself interested in other things, more fun things, and decide that since things are going so well, I can afford to let the details go for a short time. They will be fine, I will get to them soon, don't be so anal. Then the details begin to build, and build, and there are more and more interesting things to go deal with—important stuff that demands my attention right now! Crisis! Don't bother me with that right now, can't you see how busy I am? Pretty soon I am a run-away train. I certainly am not bored anymore! Now my life is more than exciting, but it does not feel like fulfillment.

Suddenly I had a very good understanding of the easiest way to get the result I wanted: not skipping a single step. Completion. The key to completion is not more intensity, longer hours and working harder. Do that very long and that spells burn-out! No, the key to completion is to teach myself the easiest way to be complete. When it is painfully obvious and well understood that skipping that step or putting it off until later will triple my work, then I finally learn the right way to be lazy.

My extremely anal friend was right. He is lazy. And that means I must utter words I dread even more than death and taxes—I was wrong!

The Magic Chuckle

by Elisabeth Revell

My mother often tells the story about The Magic Chuckle. "Somewhere in each of us there's a magic chuckle that lightens life. It probably is hidden right beneath the place where we see the absolute perfection of the way things are at any given time. The closer we are to the level of acceptance that what is, is, the greater the chance the chuckle has to be aired. The more resistant we are, the less chance the chuckle has."

One summer I found the meaning of the story.

When my boyfriend of four years unexpectedly broke up with me, I was devastated. I tried very hard to think of some sour grapes to help me get over him. It was not easy, as I thought he was close to being perfect. One I did come up with was that I really wanted to travel, he rarely did. (I was really reaching.)

So I planned a month-long trip to Europe. I had wanted to take a trip like this for many years, but didn't have anyone to go with. Now I decided to brave it alone. It became a show of my independence.

A few weeks before my trip I spoke with my former beau. In an attempt to at least save the friendship we had, we had been working on communications between us. He seemed a bit reserved, so I pushed for a little more from him, and he told me that he and his girlfriend were planning a trip to Europe. What girlfriend? When? Not only was he dating somebody, but he was traveling to Europe with her and at the same time I was going! Now I realized that it wasn't that my boyfriend didn't want to travel, but he didn't want to travel WITH ME. In an instant, my picture of myself as a cool, brave loner changed to a lonely loser. My daring European adventure would be marred by constantly wondering what they were doing. I did not find the chuckle in that.

I considered canceling the trip, but everything was in place, so off I went. As I traveled, I spoke to as many people as possible, making friends along the way. By the time I got to Switzerland, I was half-way through my trip and getting pretty used to being alone. From Geneva I went to Lucerne, a remote town in the Alps. It was the most beautiful, peaceful place I had been. I took a fabulous boat trip around the lake seeing scenes that I thought only existed in train sets. I was feeling really good. After dressing for dinner, I walked out of the hotel and stopped to look at the lovely river it was set on. It started to drizzle. I was scanning the view when my heart stopped ... there they were.

What was I supposed to do now? Should I yell, "Hey, over here!" or should I hide? I was still deciding when they started across the street toward me. I waved. He stopped dead in his tracks. At first, all he could do was point at me, and explain to his girlfriend who I was. He handed her a key and she walked right into the hotel I was staying in. He crossed the street so we could talk. Eventually he had to go. I went on, too. I cried all the way through my solo dinner. I cried all through the night, picturing them two floors below me.

The next morning I forced myself to get up and set out for a day of sight seeing. When I walked out of my hotel, the previous evening flashed before my eyes. Then I burst into laughter. I thought of the circumstances, the irony, and the unbelievable story I had to tell my friends when I got home.

I had found the magic chuckle, and with it, my independence.

Don't Fence Me In

by Trish van Vianen

Adventure travel is a passion of mine. I like navigating in the great unknown, where life is slightly unsafe, and definitely unpredictable. It really gets my adrenaline and endorphins going! The challenge is to think on my feet, to meet life head-on. Everything is new, uncharted, unplanned. It is part of my sense of fulfillment to have experiences of heart-stopping action, crisis management, and dramatic attention. I call that my hunger for "high drama." My hunger propels me toward great rewards, but sometimes, it also propels me toward trouble!

Ever since I can remember (and even long before that!) I had a hunger for exploration. My family's favorite story is about my escaping the confines of my house and yard when I was only two and a half years old. We lived in this large, old-fashioned house bordered by a large verandah, and our yard was surrounded by a four foot fence. I was the middle child, with a brother three years older and a sister two years younger. Mom would put me out in the yard to play while she spent some time with the baby. She would come back downstairs only to find that in the time it took to change a diaper or make a bottle, I was gone!!!

The scary thing for Mom was there was a highway only two blocks away. I was found cruising down the street two blocks from home and taken to the Royal Canadian Mounted Police Station (this was a small town in Southern British Columbia).   The Royal Canadian Mounted Police gave me ice cream, and contacted my Mom.   Well, that was the best! Naturally, after being rewarded with ice cream, I couldn't wait to get out again. The second time Mom had the pleasure of retrieving me from the police station, she decided she needed to do something more to contain me.   She then put a harness on me and tied me to the clothesline. My brother felt sympathetic to my misery, or at least got tired of hearing my wailing, and let me go. Over the fence and away I went again! Finally Mom put the harness on me backwards, and padlocked it onto me. She couldn't believe how easily I could get over that fence! To this day she has never figured it out (it remains top secret).

My history of searching and exploring, despite the exasperation of those around me, didn't stop there. As I got bigger, so did my need to explore. By the time I was 12, I was building snow forts for wilderness camping, and I would go off alone for 2 or 3 days in 20 degrees below zero weather. I loved the excitement and challenge of these adventures.

Nowadays I fulfill my hunger for exploration, excitement and challenge in a variety of ways. I love to swim under waterfalls and climb the Himalayas. I ski, and camp, and take mini-trips around my home base. I've learned to take risks with people, by being vulnerable and real instead of running away.   Rather than feeling tied down, my commitments to those I love have freed me to live out my dreams, make a difference in people's lives, and share my love of adventure with people I love. There is plenty of drama in meeting life head-on, full bore, no holding back, wherever I am right now.

The Pamper Pole

by Mardig Sheridan

I like to say that unless my next step gives me charge or a little fear, it's probably not big enough. Hence, several years ago I attended a "high ropes" course. Since I was very afraid of heights, this was a stretch for me.

I spent the first three prep days in terror of the events. So much so, that on the evening prior to the actual course events, I informed the class of my fear. I hoped the class would rise as one and say, "Oh, yeah, us too!" Alas, it was not to be. They all looked at me sympathetically and assured me that it was all right. I spent the night awake, imagining the agonies of the next day. After all, my image was at stake here. And so were my beloved bones and organs. Finally, at 4:30 a.m., in resignation and fear, I decided I was not going to do the course.

At 6:00 a.m. the teams gathered and I informed them I would not be participating. They assured me that was okay, and asked me to come along anyway. As we trooped off into the woods, the ropes leader stopped our group and described the first event: ascend a 35-foot branchless tree, alight on a small, flat, movable dish and swivel 180 degrees. Then we were to dive off into nothingness and catch a trapeze that was suspended from another tree top! "Ha, ha," I chuckled.

Silence greeted our arrival in the clearing. Our eyes gazed upward at this impossibly slim tree with the little dish perilously perched atop on one side, and the trapeze of doom dangling on the other side. Now it was time to learn how to harness each other. The ropes leader suggested that the first volunteer should be the one who was the most afraid. My arm flew up into the air of its own volition. I gazed in horror at the offending appendage. This couldn't be MY arm that had betrayed me! In seconds I had gone from coward of the county to Dr. Strangelove!

Before I knew it, the harness was on me. I stood there trembling, not hearing a word of the instructions, certain only of my impending death. Terror mounting, I climbed up the ladder-type strips that had been attached to the tree, and still terrified, arrived at the top. Far below me were my teammates cheering and urging me on. "Okay," I said to myself, "I'll pretend that I'm trying to get up on the dish, and then fall. I'll be lowered down to the ground and be safe once more." A little less dignified, perhaps, but with bones and brain and image intact. After all, I had climbed higher than I had ever expected. I still looked good. This would be enough.

By now my teammates were chanting my name and doing some kind of improvised dance around the tree. I felt empowered by their support. How could I bail out on them? How could I bail out on me?

I determined then and there that the only way I was going down was if the tree came with me! After several unsuccessful attempts to get on the dish, I heard the leader's voice filter up to me. "Mardig, put one foot on the dish and stand up." I did. I can only describe that incredible feeling in diametrically opposed terms: exhilarating peace. Calmly I turned around on this swiveling dish atop the violently vibrating tree, bent my knees, and dived off, catching the trapeze.

Hanging 35 feet in the air by one hand, laughing and crying at the same time, I waved ecstatically to my teammates. They responded by performing yet another impromptu acknowledgment while on their backs. I wanted that moment to last forever.

All my life I had done just enough to be seen, just enough to protect my image, just enough to convince myself that if I really wanted to do something, I could. Never once had I been willing to go the distance, to risk it all, to truly succeed. On the other side of that wall of fear I found the joy of being alive.

Washing My Image Away

by Cindy Barlow

In this media-conscious society, I've heard that having a nice glossy 8x10 image is something highly desired. I disagree. For me, being worried about my image means I am putting on a mask, worrying how I look or sound to another person, making my value subject to what they think of me. When my brain is distracted in this way, it is impossible for me to be completely engaged with the other person, and my chances for experiencing a genuine sense of aliveness are greatly reduced. I consider this a waste of my energy and a lost opportunity, because I love being highly involved with other people.

I believe this with all my heart, and had been working hard on the intellectual level to store that mask away and be my "100% real" self, 100% of the time. Perhaps I was not as close to this achievement as I thought, because I had the opportunity to acquire a little more emotional ownership, which in my case, usually shows up in some rather humbling form.

So it was that I arrived at my family's summer home, an island sanctuary in the St. Lawrence River, in June of '95. I was looking forward to a summer of peace, quiet and reflection—a time set aside for reading and writing and sorting out some of life's more difficult decisions. I had four whole days to myself before I made my first presentation in Ottawa.

Since I was the first to arrive for the season, I got the job of "opening up" the cabin. This involved everything from "airing out" to "stocking up" and, of course, activating the sources of water and power. Ah, the water pump: giver of long, leisurely bathtimes, and hot tea for sipping, not to mention those other polite little necessities that go on in the bathroom and the kitchen. I couldn't wait for my nice, relaxing stay to begin.

Alas, no key. The sun began to set as I continued to search in vain all around the area where the key was SUPPOSED to be. As the darkness grew, so did my impatience. I decided to break in through the window. So much for security! Next, lighting. No power. Cabin 3, me 0. Off to find the candles. Now for the water pump. Nothing there, either. I grabbed a flashlight and a big wrench and rooted around the outdoors pump house acting like I'd done this a million times. And ... nothing. You guessed it: zippo, zilch, nada. No water. No toilets. No showers. All of a sudden four days alone sounded like a prison sentence.

Meet Cindy Barlow, pioneer woman. Four days of doing what a bear does in the woods, taking sitz baths and doing kitchen dishes in the freezing cold water, my hopes of making a stellar impression on the folks in Ottawa were dampened, to say the least. After transporting the water pump and myself by boat and car to civilization, I arrived at the hotel with greasy hands and questionable shorts. I ironed my "official" clothes on the floor of the hotel room, and changed in the tiny ladies room in the hall. It was as I arranged my hair in the minuscule mirror that I realized there was no longer any reason to entertain any notions of protecting my "image."

Dirty or clean, in shorts or a business suit, I was the same person after all. I was Cindy Barlow, full-time genuine person, part-time pioneer woman. I was made of some pretty good stuff. I felt INVINCIBLE. Suddenly the room (and my life!) was filled with an air of openness and genuineness, with a side of delicious laughter. That is the Cindy Barlow that stays with me to this day.

Whenever I find my brain wandering towards that other Cindy, the one with the mask-like image, I picture myself squatting on the side of the riverbank, washing soap off my hands and holding my breath against the freezing cold, and I remember Cindy Barlow, pioneer woman. She can do anything. Especially laugh.

Up Against the Wall

by Mara Vizzutti

Recently I took up rock climbing at the urging of a friend. It sounded so simple: a foot here, a hand there, up, up, and away. And after all, we would be in the "safe" environment of an indoors climbing facility. This facility had climbing walls with various levels of difficulty. Having a fear of heights, they all looked like the same degree of difficulty to me—damned scary.

But what are you going to do when you're already suited up, harnessed in, and the guy who talked you into this is right beside you, grinning from ear to ear? My old friend Dave is telling me to put one foot here, one hand there, and go. Just go.

Up I go on my first attempt. I quickly learn that looking down is not an option. I got only six feet off the ground when I announced, "I'm coming down, Dave." He let me down.

On my next attempt, I climbed higher, and I experienced fear in every pore of my body. I was stuck to this wall like Spiderman. "I'm coming down, Dave," I yelled.

He replied, "Are you sure? Why don't you just sit there and think about it?"

"Sure, Dave. (Expletive deleted). I have nothing else to do but hang here and think. Thanks for your concern, Dave." However, Dave was right about one thing—I had a lot of things to think about. Things like trust. Like falling. Like my place in the universe. And falling. I wondered how the equipment was holding up. I wondered how my muscles were holding up. I wondered about my trust in Dave. I wondered how I looked hanging there—stuck, afraid, and with Dave still down there grinning. Seconds seemed like hours, and I noticed I still wasn't moving. None of these burning questions were propelling me up the wall. Uncomfortable as I was with these issues, I was more uncomfortable just physically hanging there. Dave, still grinning, waited for me to get past it.

So I did. I climbed on. By the end of the evening I had reached the top and touched the ceiling! Hail the conquering hero, it's party time! A feeling of great relief and exhilaration swept over me.

"Now," says Dave, "comes the fun part. Mara Vizzutti, come on down!"

Believe it or not, I heard myself reply, "Dave, I'm not coming down." Not when I realized his idea of "coming down" was rappelling from the top, nothing to hold onto but a little rope, while I enjoyed a full experience of the height I had finally attained. Talk about your leap of faith!

Eventually I determined, once more, that as uncomfortable as it may be to try something new, to look silly, or even be scared (in public yet!); how much worse it would be just to hang there out in space, afraid to move up or down.

Trust me. Thanks to Dave, I know. A little faith gets you past the toughest walls.

Outside the Zone

by Dan Haygeman

The first time I jumped out of an airplane, I knew that my ripcord would automatically be pulled for me, and that my reserve chute would deploy on its own if my main chute failed. I also knew that the pilot was good at his job and was competent to tell me when to climb out on the strut in preparation to jump.

My job seemed fairly simple, especially when I practiced it on the ground. Bob The Jumpmaster would tap me on the shoulder. I was to climb out onto the tire of the aircraft, and hang on to the wing strut until Bob's next signal. At that point I was to jump in the air, swing my body horizontal, push myself back away from the airplane ... and let go. I was breathing hard at the prospect, but felt fairly confident except for the very last step: letting go.

So much for rehearsal. The first thing I noticed when the pilot actually started the engine was a much more intense rush of sensation. Taking off in a light plane with the door removed is a whole different experience, especially since the student is the one sitting on the floor next to that gaping opening. The roar of the engine, the smell of the exhaust and the rush of the grass runway blend in an overwhelming explosion of intensity. This was way more of everything than I had anticipated.

I did climb out on the tire when signaled. I saw the ground 3,000 feet below me and wondered when the signal to die would come. When Bob The Jumpmaster leaned out toward me, cupped his hands, and yelled "Now!" I had a curious experience. I've heard it described as 'a sudden drop in IQ.' My mind dumped the entire contents of my short, long and medium-term memory. "Let go!" Bob yelled. "What?" I earnestly replied. At that moment the reality of all that I had embarked upon became crystal clear, and like the proverbial deer in the headlights, I froze.

Bob leaned way out, looked me square in the eyes, slapped me on the thigh and screamed "Now" in a voice that would have intimidated even the mechanical tyrannosaur in "Jurassic Park." Somehow I funneled the energy of his commitment to me and to what I had chosen, into the part of me that flicks the switch from 'thinking about it' to 'action.' I jumped. I swung horizontal. I pushed back. I even let go. And when the chute opened, I regained my conscious mind. I opened my eyes. I was in bliss.

It never would have happened without Jumpmaster Bob. In letting go of that airplane, I realized I had let go of the only security I had in that moment. Only my prior commitment to act in accordance with the agreements I had made with my coach made the difference. I was lucky to have had Bob as a coach, because the moves I was required to make for success were far outside the "comfort zone" from which I normally evaluate potential actions. Left to my own standard operating mode, I'd still be clinging to that Cessna.

Within the safe and known habitual patterns of my "comfort zone," I'm somehow comfortable even if miserable. When I step even briefly outside my comfort zone, I am not usually very attractive or elegant. The terrors I actually experience in leaving the familiar are always greater than I can prepare for by anticipating the risks. I can reassure or anesthetize my present ego all I want with rehearsal, visualization, chocolate, or whatever, but the fact is, from my ego's perspective, anytime I talk about changing the rules by which I live my life, I am talking about my ego's apparent death: the death of who I think I am.

Coaching supports such death-defying action in this way: I grant limited authority to a coach to guide my actions in particular areas of my life. In doing this, I am committing to choose actions based on a separate, strange, even alien intelligence (that of my coach) without modulating them with the endless self-reinforcing internal dialogue by which I define myself.

Most of the time I do not catch myself in my own unconscious patterns. A better strategy: get completely involved in doing what I have committed to do, and watch out for the obvious signs that I am entering new territory: (feeling angry, defensive, confused, etc.). Such symptoms can act as a kind of warning signal that a boundary of my present comfort zone is being threatened. This is the time to engage in a conversation about what is occurring for me with a coach and/or people I trust and who are committed to my success. Out of the self-acceptance and support generated in those conversations, I am more ready to take that next step, evaluate the result, and continue to move forward.

I sometimes like to remind myself: no one pays the circus to watch the trapeze people swing back and forth; the real thrills are in letting go.

When You Wish Upon A Star

by Judy Revell

In an informal survey I conducted, I found that it's an almost universal desire of parents to have their children develop good posture habits. This survey came about when I told my physical therapist that my back was beginning to hurt. Having an aching back isn't good for anyone. For someone who spends most of her awake time in a wheelchair, this is really not good. Sitting straight, I'm told, is part of the solution. When my physical therapist told me that I needed to pay special attention to how I sit, it immediately brought up memories of my childhood.

I remembered my mother telling me to sit up straight, and her stories of how my grandmother had learned good posture. Nails were partially pounded into a long board, and then this board was propped up behind my grandmother whenever she sat down. She would get pricked if ever she should slump. That story paints quite a vivid picture, doesn't it? But most of all, I recalled my father saying "Shoulders back, chest out, stomach in, head up."

During my childhood and young adulthood it got so I heartily disliked hearing the advice about having good posture. I seldom paid it long-term attention, which is probably why it was said so often. Of course, "often" is a relative term, especially to a child. "Shoulders back, chest out, stomach in, head high" could have been repeated several times a day or only a few times a year. Still, it was "often" to me.

I don't have particularly good posture today. In fact, it's horrible—based on the result that my back is beginning to hurt. I guess sitting straight hasn't been important enough. Well, at least, not to me. I really should sit up straight. I've been told that again and again, but until it is my desire, and I'm the one who focuses on it for myself, there's little chance of that happening. It needs to become what I call a "shooting star" desire.

Do you remember hearing about wishes and shooting stars? If you make a wish when you see a falling star, the wish will come true. In the words of Jimminy Cricket, "When you wish upon a star, your dreams come true." Wishing on the star is only part of the story. The wish will only come true if it is made before the star disappears. For those who have seen a falling star, you know how quickly it appears and disappears. To make and complete a wish before the star disappears, the wish must have been in the forefront of consciousness—not only just at that moment, but generally.

Whichever desire we give most of our time and attention to is the "wish" that will manifest. It is only a matter of time ... and investment.

Are you ready for your next falling star?

Walking on Broken Glass

by Bobby Ng

A world of difference lies between thinking something might be important and knowing that it is. When I merely think something might be important, my attention is distracted by the obstacle in front of me; as if I were barefoot and I see shards of broken glass scattered all over the ground between me and what I think I want. I need clarity and commitment to propel me over that broken glass.

You see, I've always been a big believer in keeping my options open. "Commitment"—that was that Big "C" word, one of those scary words I rarely even said out loud. Then I heard this quote from Martin Buber that really gave me something to think about. He said, "I am the sum of my commitments." Well, I wasn't making any commitments. What did that say about me?

So I started making commitments—some big, some small—and then watched the difference. When considering an invitation of a friend, I would usually say "I'll see," meaning, "I'll see what time I wake up" or "I'll see if something more appealing turns up." I had said that I wanted intimacy in my life, that I believed it was important to recharge, grow, move forward. So I started changing my responses to: "Let's go. Here's my money. Buy me a ticket." Or, "Our friendship is important. I am committed to it."

I had always maintained that a close, loving relationship with "the right one" was important to me.

But in my relationships, I would keep my foot in the doorway, so to speak, because ... well, what if it's not the right one? What if something better comes along? I realized that by keeping my foot in the door, I wasn't exactly as free as I thought to go after what I said I wanted.

At the time I was discovering these things, I was working as a deejay at a radio station. One day out of the blue I got a call at work from a stranger. "I just wanted to say how much I enjoy your company on the drive home," she said. Something about what she was saying...something about her tone of voice... something prompted me to keep her on the line as long as I could. In between commercials and my on-air patter our conversation moved to an annual charity fund-raiser I did. "Will you have it this year?" she asked. "I wouldn't mind making a pledge."

"I'll call you," replied this rocket scientist. "What's your number?" As I often say...slow I may be, stupid I'm not.

I phoned for her pledge, then asked if she'd like to meet. So we met and talked..and talked some more..and ..by our third meeting it was quite clear to me. Time to say some scary words. That "Big C" word, for starters. And was I scared? You better believe it. In retrospect I had at least two fears: fear of failure—what if she says no? And fear of success—what if she says yes?

I wouldn't say what I was feeling was courage, but I sure had clarity, I simply saw what I wanted. I wanted what I saw. I knew. So with fear in my heart, and my heart in my throat, I stepped on that broken glass.

Incidentally, we got married in 1991.

Passing the Favor On

by Diane Kennedy

Years ago I went into the hospital for some major surgery. The long and the short of it is, it didn't go well. I started hemorrhaging. I puffed up like the Pillsbury doughboy. It was a week or more before I began to feel any better.

Just when I started to feel human again, I began to get visits from many of my friends. One Sunday afternoon, one of the Sunday school teachers from my church brought her children in with her to visit me. They had made me cards and things, and it was very nice. On the next day, this same girl came back alone, and she offered to wash my hair.

Now, being a woman who had been in the hospital, untouched and unmoved for about a week, I looked like death warmed over. My hair was especially awful. The Sunday school teacher explained that once she had been in the hospital, and somebody had offered this same service to her. She wheeled me down the hall to the shower area and washed my hair. I didn't even know this woman very well, yet I felt extraordinarily special to have received this gift.

Years later I had the opportunity to visit our minister's wife in the hospital. She was pregnant and experiencing some complications. I felt compelled to come visit her every day, even though I didn't know her very well. I would bring little presents, grab bags, books. I just felt drawn to do that, and I didn't really understand why.

The minister's wife and I were in a class together some six months later, and we talked about those visits in the hospital. She said, "Diane, I've been thinking about your visits while I was in the hospital, I have realized that you were there for you as much as you were for me." The moment she said it, I knew it was absolutely true. I had felt drawn to visit this woman because of the gift that I had received.

Someone had given to me unconditionally. In that simple gift of washing my hair, I had also received the gift of wanting to pass the favor on. Each of us is given so much, in so many ways, in the course of our lives. It's not so much about giving back in kind to the person who had given to you, but about continuing to give to other people all our lives as we see the need arise. Gifts of time and caring are the most priceless gifts of all.

A Second Chance

by Dan Sullivan

I am nervous about taking my little cat, Friar Tuck (Tucky), to the vet today. Her mom, Gypsy, had similar symptoms, and didn't come back. I chose to put Gypsy to sleep rather than have her suffer. Gypsy had been with me for 21 years.

Loud meowing tells me that Tucky wants out of the cat carrier. She keeps "talking" to me as she always has, but this time she is shouting. Even though I am worried she will hurt herself if she is out of the carrier, I listen to her; immediately she jumps in my lap and purrs. My heart is aching. I don't want to lose her.

My best friend of 22 years has a kidney disease. The vet explains that she isn't suffering now and could possibly live for several more months; but she will need a special diet and daily shots which I will have to administer. My best friend won't suffer and I have a second chance to complete with her before she dies. What a gift for both of us.

We play fetch, our favorite game of many years. And Tucky sleeps on the pillow next to me. Time is limited. This is the only moment that exists. Every moment I love her to pieces; I remember our fun times and the silly things she has done to make me laugh.

Although Tucky has been stable now for several months, I don't let up on loving her and cherishing every moment together. I know she is more important to me than a rug or how my house smells or what my friends think.

Tucky and I have earned nearly another year to be together since that day I first learned of her illness. Now it is clear that Tucky's time has come. I take her to the vet immediately, knowing that nothing more can be done. My journal entry for September 4, 1994 begins: "Good-bye, my friend. Thank you for your spirit and your gift of unconditional love."

It has been three years since that day, and I still miss Tucky. Her spirit lives with me, and I am grateful for the extra time we had together. I made the most of every moment. In doing so, I am no longer the same person I was prior to that last year. For someone who has lived most of his life in his head, my little cat reached in and touched my heart.

The Decision to Forgive

by Cindy Barlow

How do you know, deep inside, when forgiveness has really taken place? What does it mean to be "complete" with someone or thing? I believe that true forgiveness produces a particular feeling. I suggest that it is by this feeling that we can measure whether we've really finished what we set out to do. Forgiveness doesn't require the assistance of the person you wish to be complete with, it's only about you. And when you have truly, completely forgiven, new energy is available. for the present.

I am the eldest of six children, which means that I have logged many miles in the diaper changing department. Being the oldest also meant I was expected to set a good example (i.e., "Be more obedient and less trouble than your younger siblings, because I already have enough to handle!") Much of that message was passed on by my father, a brilliant but rather controlling man. For instance, in my freshman year at college, when I wanted to switch majors, my father enrolled me in a week-long series of aptitude tests to determine exactly what I should study!

You see, I had a great many interests and tended to jump from one thing to another. This personality trait irritated my father to no end. He believed you should pick one thing, stick with it and succeed at it. Period. Nevertheless, I had a series of very entertaining jobs, and found myself drawn to a variety of learning situations, leaving each one with the newest and hottest "fix-it" idea for my family. My family, and my father in particular, didn't especially like being "fixed." Not surprisingly, our time together at holidays and such seemed to be strained and tension-filled. All I really wanted was my father's approval.

When I became a parent myself, I realized that I was learning parenting from raising my oldest child, just as my father had learned with me. I also began to see the value of forgiving my father for doing the best he could at the time he raised me, because, based on results, he'd done a good job.

I remember the intense feelings of release, relief and lightness which accompanied my decision to forgive. It was a feeling too good not to share! I called my father to tell him I loved him . When he answered, his voice was tight with emotion. "Thanks for calling, honey, I love you, too."

Those were the very last words I ever heard my father speak. He died suddenly just a few weeks later from a tragic fall.

His funeral, while far from a happy occasion, was one of the most fulfilling times of my life. I was able to honor and celebrate his life as I said good-bye. I felt alive, grateful, at peace—and complete.

Counting On Time

by Bobby Ng

Something is not quite right, I thought, but what ...?

I knew I wasn't 100%, but I couldn't put a finger on what exactly was wrong. I hesitate to call it nausea, but I had the most peculiar feeling of unwellness. And there was this headache—for lack of a better word—that wasn't a sharp pain nor a dull throbbing sensation either. It was sort of a stuffed up, heavy feeling, I guess.

I was beginning to have to guess about a lot of things. It was the first night of a 4-day course I was facilitating, and instead of the usual "Gung Ho!" endorphin rush, life began to look just a little fuzzy, a bit unreal. Mostly I was forgetful. Actually, forgetful is a an understatement! Not only had I forgotten some things I wanted to say, I also forgot things I had already said, right after I said them. And after I'd said them again. I must have gotten through that first night on auto-pilot, because I did not (and still do not) remember much of what took place that night. People told me I repeated some things four times. I know repetition is valuable, but ...

At the end of the course I flew home and had a little visit with my doctor. He suggested a CT scan, and it showed that I had suffered a stroke—a brain hemorrhage. That certainly grabbed my attention, believe me! If the bleeding had been heavier, or an inch or two in another direction, that might have been my final curtain call.

We do not have an unlimited charge account with time, I like to say when I'm on-stage. Now I have had a major opportunity to review those words and to ask myself, do I practice what I teach? I do know that there's a fine line between planning for the future and putting off for the future. I'm taking another look at where I draw the line.

Trout Run

by Leigh Farrell

Trout Run, Pennsylvania was one of those almost mythical, idyllic towns where kids like me grew up exploring the woods or wading the streams that meandered through town, or using the whole geography of the town to play capture the flag. In winter we sledded the hills and in summer we built brush forts and scooped up slimy polliwogs with glee. We welcomed every hand and glove at pick-up baseball games too, no matter how young or old—because in our town there could be no game without everyone.

My older brother and I attended the classic brick, two-room schoolhouse where each kid 'helped' the kids in the grade behind and got put in their places by those in the grade ahead. Our teacher, like our building, was an antique—a long-retired saint who volunteered for this backwater elementary school where the furnace still had to be stoked each morning. Her temper was as short as her humor, however, and so none of us escaped solitary confinement in the frigid cloakroom for the usual "frog in the desk" or "ink in the milk" classroom diversions. My class of eleven was the largest in the school, eight larger than the one ahead, and I had seven cousins in six grades. It was hard being bad anonymously.

My loving parents knew the benefits of having us hoe the garden sometimes when we wanted to play, snap beans when we wanted to swim, and do the dishes when we would rather be doing anything else. By keeping a garden, canning and freezing, sewing clothes and splitting wood, they taught us that supper doesn't just come from the store and heat from the furnace; and that not much will happen in this world unless we plant a seed, wield a hoe, swing an ax and work up some sweat.

Each person in Trout Run was unique, a character without peer. Old Bud Hoolihan, who was not quite 'right' in the head, kept us safe crossing the road to school and scared the bejeepers out of us on Halloween. Mildred Flemming, the spinster only-child of the local doctor, who nursed him quietly and gracefully until it was his time to die, sang off-key alto in the back of the church every Sunday. Uncle Dean was the tight-lipped Justice of the Peace, president of the Fire Hall, and the name to drop when you got caught speeding later on. Ruby-haired Fran Stoudt owned the general store, had a contagious laugh, and dispensed licorice sticks on credit for kids who probably still owe her.

There were about 196 other characters in town, but you get the picture. We lived the innocence of youth, surrounded with love and care from every one.

I left Trout Run at seventeen, bored with small towns and ready to experience "real" life. I've learned a bit—at universities, school in Europe, doctoral studies— since those two-room schoolhouse days, but nothing as important as the lessons from that small town...

> that each person is unique, quirky and wonderfully fine, just as they are, and important to the whole
> that nature and people are connected, deeply
> that we're all connected, really,
> and that love—joyful acceptance—is the most meaningful gift we have to give and to receive.
> Maybe that's all I ever really need to know.

The White Feather Award

by Randy Revell

As far back as I can remember the main theme in my life has been that of strengthening good will. I didn't use those words, but that's what I attempted to create. For me, good will includes kindness, unselfishness, respect, brotherly love, empathy, concern, friendliness and hospitality. It is a kindly feeling, both toward one's self and others. You can probably imagine the flak I took, as a child, for being this way.

The first big realization about the importance of good will to me happened when I was twelve years old. I was in a two-week YMCA-sponsored summer camp for boys near Medford Lakes, New Jersey. We lived in cabins that were not much more than tents with double bunk beds along both walls. The bunks were made with canvas stretched between two 2x4's. I slept in one of the upper bunks. There were eight boys in the cabin.

We had a bonfire ceremony the last night of camp. After dancing around the bonfire and singing, a number of awards were presented. With fanfare and solemnity I was presented with the White Feather award for demonstrating leadership. With hindsight, I think it was more of an award for being the most orderly camper. Regardless, it was a big deal. I felt proud to receive it.

Two of my cabin-mates didn't like the fact that I won the White Feather award. Although my memory is fuzzy, I think one of them thought he should have won it. I remember clearly that he was bigger than me—and a bully. That night, after lights out, with everyone else asleep, the bully and his buddy woke me up. He had his pocketknife in his hand with the big blade extended. He said, "You think you're such a big deal. You're not, because you're gutless. You're afraid to push this knife through the bunk." (Our cabin counselor had made a point about not damaging the canvas on the bunks.)

Well, I tried to worm out of it. I used reason and logic. But I was trapped in my emotions. I was afraid of the bully and what he might do to me if I didn't do what he wanted me to do. To prove that I had guts and would do something that would be disapproved of by the counselor, I pushed the knife blade through the canvas.

This was significant to me at the time. With what I learned from the experience, it remains so. I don't remember much of what happened afterward. I don't even remember if the counselor saw the very small cut. What I do remember is lying in my bunk with many silent tears. I was ashamed of myself—ashamed for giving in to my fear, and even more ashamed of committing an act of destruction. I cried and cried—and made sure no one heard me.

I also remember the feeling of great resolve that came to me later in the night. A resolve to be constructive, to be strong, to stand up to bullying. And, most important, to strive for good will.

The Story Tellers

Cindy Barlow

Energetic, enthusiastic and compassionate, the charismatic Ms. Barlow believes that inspiring others is her life's purpose.

Cindy Barlow's diverse educational background includes studies at Johns Hopkins University in Art, French, and the workings of the human mind. Cindy's professional experiences are equally as varied. She began her career as a buyer for a chain of department stores in Baltimore, Maryland. In the publishing world, Cindy held positions of both Operations Manager and Assistant Sales Manager. She honed her public speaking and training skills working with various direct marketing companies. During a career hiatus, Cindy raised two sons and taught aerobics, before joining a consulting firm.

Area Manager for Baltimore from 1989 - 1990, Cindy Barlow became a Program Leader with Context Associated in 1994.

Cindy's interests include tennis and sewing, and being an "amazing" bridge player. She is passionate about water, trees, puppies and chocolate of any kind. Cindy and her husband Timothy live near the shore of Lake Ontario in Toronto.

Cindy's belief in full participation from the top down is evident in her stories "Washing My Image Away", and "The Decision to Forgive." She brings a lively example of the "up close and personal" style of teaching and sharing.

Here are a few personal additions to her biography.

Who or what makes you laugh loudest and longest? My husband. Robin Williams is a close second.

What is your idea of perfect happiness? Heaven to me is a Caribbean beach with lots of sunshine, a temperature of 80 degrees Fahrenheit, a good book—oh, and a Piña Colada machine nearby.

What do you value most in your friends? Honesty, trust and a sense of humor.

What was your wildest, most dangerous or most unique experience? Definitely not printable!

What is your next big goal? To develop and implement a program to assist people in trusting themselves even more.

What novel, film, or person has influenced you the most? "Many Masters, Many Lives" by Dr. Brian L. Weiss.

What is your primary leadership style? I am a promoter. In one of my programs I was so involved and animated during a discussion that I failed to notice that the top two buttons on my blouse had come undone. The blouse had only three buttons.

Who are your heroes in real life? Carl Jung, C.S. Lewis, Bette Midler, Jesus.

What one world problem would you like to have the most impact on? People's willingness to trust themselves and others.

What is your most treasured possession? I no longer have any, having pared down my belongings.

What is your motto? Paint word pictures so that the blind can see.

Kathleen Carie

Kathleen Carie, along with her five brothers, was born and raised in Fairbanks, Alaska. Deciding that 18 years of 40 degrees below zero weather was mind-numbingly enough, she migrated south to Seattle, Washington and graduated from Seattle University with a degree in Hospital Administration.

Believing that management is management, Kathleen took her administrative skills to the restaurant business in 1975, running two of Seattle's biggest and most popular hotspots: Jake O'Shaughnessey's and F.X. McRory's. One of the highlights of those nine years as one of Seattle's few women managers in the restaurant business was a column written about her that appeared in The Seattle Times; another was appearing in a LeRoy Neiman painting, commissioned for the back of the bar!

Kathleen joined Context Associated in 1983 as Special Projects Manager. She helped design the company's initial sales training, then developed (and took) the position of Graduate Manager, and introduced The Walk in 1985. Kathleen was a member of the Implementation Team, became The Advancement of Excellence Product Manager, and has been leading programs for 13 years. Another of Kathleen's many roles is that of Regional Manager for Seattle, Portland, Ottawa, and Toronto.

Well-known and well-loved for her brash, irreverent sense of humor and outrageous high-stepping energy, Kathleen Carie can occasionally be found enjoying her beautiful home, a host of equally loud friends, or enjoying being seen in a neighborhood pub.

Kathleen admits that being front and center, in a red dress no less, in a LeRoy Neiman painting is a pretty unique experience -- something that (in her own words) "only me, Frank Sinatra and the Playboy girls" can boast having. She admires Bette Midler and anyone else who can turn big talk into big dreams come true. One thing it took Kathleen a while to make happen was her lifestyle change to non-smoker, a story she shares with us in "Up in Smoke."

Catching up with this whirlwind of activity was no mean feat, so here are the few pearls of wisdom we managed to catch before she was on the move again.

If you were cloned, what would your duplicate be doing right now? Serving my every need.

Who or what makes you laugh loudest and longest? Talking dirty with my best friends!

What is your idea of heaven on earth? Dialing my voicemail and hearing it say I have no new messages! This has never happened in my lifetime.

What do you value most in your friends? Humor, irreverence, honesty, and having a hell of a good time.

What is your greatest extravagance? My "no limit" shopping. I once went out to buy a refrigerator and came home with a briefcase for the same price. I said to myself, "Who cares? I don't cook!" To this day I still introduce my briefcase as my refrigerator.

What is your primary leadership style? Promoting controller! Any questions? I am the master delegator— and I say aloud what most people only dare to think!

What is your current fantasy about the future? Enough money to retire in style.

What does your personal life look like? Private .... and very juicy!

How do you keep it fresh? I use deodorant! And I don't sweat the small stuff. I find humor in everything, and see the magic chuckle in life.

What do you consider to be your greatest accomplishment? I put myself through school and I own my own, beautiful home. But that's not it. My greatest accomplishment is getting up everyday, excited about life, ready to have more and do more. It is my energy, enthusiasm and aliveness.

What is your most treasured possession? Certainly my dad's gold coin is one. The love and respect of all my friends is my real treasure.

What about your work keeps you coming back? Autonomy and freedom. Fun things like assisting people in creating their life's dreams. I really believe there are no greener pastures out there. I can create anything I want, be as successful as I want to be. We get to run our own show. I'll probably be here till I die. Why would I want to go anywhere else?

What is your motto? Who can I empower now?

Catherine Elliott

Born in Marysville, California, Catherine Elliott grew up in San Luis Obispo and received her B.A. in English Literature from the University of California at Santa Barbara.

Catherine moved to Olympia, Washington in 1980 and became the state's first Executive Director of the Battered Women's Network. Testifying in front of the state legislature was one of the highlights of her 8-year career as an advocate for these "wonderful and heartbreaking" women and children.

Ms. Elliott's next post was in the Washington Governor's office, researching both the environmental and job impact issues regarding the preservation of the Spotted Owl. Catherine also conducted a scientific research project with ten of the nation's top Ph.D.'s on the protection of old growth forests. She is currently a manager with Washington State's Department of Natural Resources, where her responsibilities include resource planning for five million acres of state land.

Catherine was introduced to Context Associated's programs while working in the Governor's office. She began assisting in 1993, coaching in 1995, and acts as a Program Leader as well.

Ms. Elliott enjoys old movies, walking and running, and watching wildlife with her husband from the deck of their home.

"Dreams do come true," admits Catherine Elliott (author of "A Bold Step"), who adds that "heaven is birdwatching on the lake in my robe." Other local residents who visit Catherine in her heaven on earth include river otters, beaver, and osprey.

We caught Catherine in between sightings to ask her these questions.

If you were cloned, what would your duplicate be doing right now? Studying literature or biology.

Who or what makes you laugh loudest and longest? Self-awareness tinged with irony. I remember when a new boss of mine described herself in our first meeting as lacking a sense of humor. I burst out laughing because I was so charmed that she would admit something most people would never say. It was a funny and brave thing to say.

What is your greatest extravagance? Afternoon naps on clean, crisp sheets. Time stops.

What do you value most in your friends? Credibility—they mean and do what they say; candor—I know where they stand; realistic optimism—I'm very drawn to optimistic people who know the full picture and still choose to find out how it will work. I don't buy it if someone comes to their optimism by ignoring what's going on.

What was your wildest, most dangerous or most unique experience? I looked up from an Alaskan sandbar at a very large black bear who was coming toward me because I was near salmon. Two people had already been killed by bears that week, but I knew this bear only wanted the fish—unless I ran. My (now) husband Tom and I walked a ridiculously slow pace away from the bear and his river. Back at the cabin, I shook from shock and grinned at the same time. I loved being that close to something that powerful and dangerous. We survived because of that bear's choice to pursue fish instead of us.

What is your next big goal? Creating a close and mature relationship with my husband. This is the scariest and newest territory I've been to yet!

Which talent would you most like to have? Patience. I want everything now. I always have.

What is your primary leadership style? I'm clearly a controller. I even attempted to take over control of a program when I was a participant. Now I acknowledge and enjoy it blatantly. I find the more I give myself permission to control, the more respectful and humorous I become.

What is your most treasured possession? Letters my mother wrote me before she died. They are the only thing in my safety deposit box.

What does your personal life look like? I have only two gears: on and off. No confusion about which one I'm in. I do each of them intensely. So I "go" at home, too. I clean, organize, orchestrate, accomplish and meddle—or nothing at all. My husband, by contrast, has one gear— in the middle, which means he can generally make the leap to whichever gear I'm in.

I also tend to blurt out whatever is in my head. I call it a deep commitment to candor. Tom calls it not having a private thought in my head. My closest friends know everything about me—all my weird ideas, fears, goofy mistakes, passions. I find it very freeing. It also helps me trust that when my friends say they love me, they know who they're loving—not an image.

How do you let off steam? I exercise like crazy on my treadmill. I watch dopey romantic movies. I chirp.

What about your work keeps you coming back? I deeply believe that each of us can make a difference—or not—our choice. I come back to make a difference.

I also come back because it's so fun and it thoroughly distracts me. It's like taking a vacation because I feel completely transported by the community we create in the program room. Then, at the end, I return home tired and satisfied.

Leigh Farrell

Leigh Farrell was born and raised in the small town of Trout Run, Pennsylvania. She participated as an American Field Exchange Student to the Netherlands in 1963-64, and was a university exchange student to France in 1967.

Leigh's educational background includes a Ph.D. in Comparative Literature from the University of Washington and a Masters degree in French languages and literature from Pennsylvania State University. She taught for four years at the University of Washington in such diverse fields as French, English, Women's Studies and Comparative Literature. She is a published poet and has written a book of literary criticism entitled: "The Archetypal Image: An Interpretation of the Poetry of Theodore Roethke, Arthur Rimbaud, W.B. Yeats and Robert Frost."

Leigh joined Context Associated in 1987, and has been leading programs ever since. Her interest in bringing the peoples of the world together for mutual understanding and peace prompted her to organize and introduce Context Associated's programs to Tashkent, Moscow, and Israel. She led three programs in Tashkent, and trained several of the Russian program leaders. In addition, Leigh and her family lived in St. Petersburg, Russia in the summer of 1994, and with a physician and his family in Tashkent, Uzbekistan, September 1987 as part of the Seattle-Tashkent Sister City Physician Exchange.

She enjoys downhill and cross-country skiing, expanding her mind, and adventuring. Previously an aficionado of rock and mountain climbing, she and her husband have kayaked in the Queen Charlotte Islands, in Hawaii, and in Florida.

Leigh Farrell lives in Seattle with her husband of 28 years, Roy, and their 17 year old son, Chad.

No one leads from the heart quite like Leigh Farrell. Whether it's love shared and experienced in the program room or in the family room, love is what keeps her coming back again and again. Leigh writes about the many loves of her life in her stories, "Trout Run", and "When Love Goes Down The Drain."

Leigh was willing to answer a variety of questions providing they all had something to do with chocolate.

If you were cloned, what would your duplicate be doing right now? Teaching at a large university, writing books on psychology and spirituality, and lecturing around the country. Or eating chocolate.

What is your idea of perfect happiness? Chocolate.

What is your greatest extravagance? Chocolate.

What do you value most in your friends? The ability to love, laugh and grow.

What was your wildest, most dangerous or most unique experience? My husband and I spent six weeks mountain climbing in the Swiss Alps in the spring of 1976. The most dangerous part was the final ice-climbing pitch on the top of the Jungfrau.

What is your current fantasy about the future? Taking our programs to Europe and the Middle East where they will spread around the world and be well known, well attended, and well appreciated. My personal goal is to develop a course on spirituality for Context Associated.

What is your primary leadership style? Who knows? I try everything.

Who are your heroes in real life? My husband, my son, my parents, Albert Schweitzer, Victor Frankl, Raoul Wallenberg, Nelson Mandela, Helen Keller, Gandhi, Isaac Rabin, Martin Luther King, Eleanor Roosevelt, Elie Wiesel, Danaan Perry, Aung San Suu Kyi and all the spiritual leaders who have ever lived.

What one world problem would you like to have the most impact on? World peace.

What piece of music most expresses your life? Beethoven's "Ode to Joy."

What does your personal life look like? A balancing act.

Are you funny at home? Do they like it? Only when I've had my chocolate.

Jeff Gaines

Jeff Gaines has a very youthful and warm presence that is both infectious and inspirational. He leads a very active and full life and is generally remembered for his sense of humor.

He was born in Milwaukee, Wisconsin, where he spent his first 13 years. He then resided in Boston, Massachusetts for seven years, where he received his Mechanical Engineering degree from the University of Massachusetts.

Jeff was introduced to Context Associated in November 1993, and has been a facilitator since February 1996. He also holds the position of Service Department Manager for Nova Networks, Inc., a service company specializing in both local and wide area computer networking.

Jeff has a number of hobbies that include playing basketball, golfing, movie going, and cookie eating. He and his wife Noel live in Seattle, Washington.

Jeff Gaines is one of the funniest engineers we know. His stories are "Children Are Natural Winners" and "The Devil's In The Details." Hope that sense of humor holds up ... at least through the following questions.

If you were cloned, what would your duplicate be doing right now? Working. I'd be golfing, skiing, or taking a cruise.

Who or what makes you laugh? I have a bit of a dark side to my humor. So sarcasm and the like work with me. I also have a very silly side. Jim Carrey in "The Mask" slayed me.

What is your idea of perfect happiness? Certain elements are a must in life for me: Intensity, challenge, nurturing, insight, humor and being the center of attention. Perfect happiness would be living all of these without all of the stress and overwork that I tend to find with them.

What is your greatest extravagance? My car. A Jeep Cherokee. I love it. The extravagant part is I tend to get a new one every 2-3 years.

What do you value most in your friends? Humor, loyalty, reliability, support and money (just kidding about the money).

What was your wildest, most dangerous or most unique experience? Wildest: Honeymoon Caribbean cruise.

Most dangerous: near death rock climbing experience where I was below the person I was climbing with, and a huge piece of rock started tumbling down the mountain at me. It then split in two right above my head and a half of the rock passed by me on either side.

Most unique: Quit my job, ended a relationship, sold my house and dropped out of grad school all in a three month period, then went golfing for a month in California.

What is your current fantasy about the future? Being financially wealthy. I'm wealthy in many ways now, but I'd like the cash.

Which talent would you most like to have? Being able to easily experience a wide range of emotions. Some of my friends call me Data (from "Star Trek").

What is your primary leadership style? I'm a supporting controller. This means I like to take charge, but don't like to hurt people's feelings. It makes for many humorous situations.

How do you keep it fresh? Zip lock bags. No, seriously, with humor. I can tell things are getting dull or too stressed when there is not enough humor.

What one world problem would you like to have the most impact on? Peace.

What is your most treasured possession? My wedding ring.

What does your personal life look like? Busy! Get back to me later. Actually, sports (mostly basketball), movies, yard/house work and an occasional night out dancing or some kind of group outing.

What about your work keeps you coming back? The challenge, working with people I like, and the future opportunities. Oh, and money. It may be shallow, but it works.

What is your motto? I've upped my standards, up yours!

Dan Haygeman

Dan Haygeman has a B.A. degree in Philosophy from Augustana College of South Dakota, a graduate degree in Psychology from Pepperdine University, and has done doctoral work at the University of Southern California.

Dan's background is in human systems with experience in administration, marketing and sales. Previous career roles have included stints as an Assistant Technical Director for KELO TV, cabin steward for Pan Am World Airways, family therapist and director of social services.

Dan is currently a Program Leader for Context Associated, and has been associated with the company in a variety of roles since 1985. In addition, Mr. Haygeman is co-founder and principal consultant of ConsultNet, a Seattle-based network of consultants, entrepreneurs and service providers.

Dan conducts human effectiveness seminars and workshops throughout the U.S. and Canada and provides consulting services designed to foster the creation of high performance in corporations and government agencies. Mr. Haygeman's article entitled "Humanizing Voice Mail" appeared in the April 1991 issue of Washington CEO magazine. He has provided customized coaching and facilitation to a wide range of individual and corporate clients: from AT&T managers to artists, musicians, psychotherapists, authors and teachers.

Dan's recreational pursuits and leisure interests include: photography, running and downhill skiing, and bee-keeping.

Besides his love for his puppy, ("Billy Bob Meets the Vet"), Dan's love of animals includes bees. He recalls a wild and dangerous experience when, while wearing boxer shorts, he forgot to tape his pant legs shut before working with his bees .... Dan tells another story of meeting danger and fear in "Outside the Zone."

Dan paused from his whirlwind of activity long enough to answer these questions.

If you were cloned, what would your duplicate be doing right now? Playing on tour with James Taylor and Marc Cohn.

Who or what makes you laugh loudest and longest? Stories about short French people in interesting sexual situations.

What is your idea of perfect happiness? My present life, whenever I'm in a mood of gratitude.

What do you value most in your friends? Humor, directness, listening and creativity.

What is your next big goal? Financial independence.

What is your primary leadership style? I am an introvert, so I don't reveal my true style.

How do you keep it fresh? Baste it with olive oil and refrigerate below 340 degrees.

Who are your heroes in real life? Christopher Reeve, Jack Kennedy, Dan Sullivan.

What one world problem would you like to have the most impact on? The disconnection and wasted energy in the world.

What is your most treasured possession? My brown 1981 Volvo with 278,000 actual miles.

What piece of music is your life most like? Bruce Hornsby—"The Show Goes On."

What about your work keeps you coming back? I love the energy of people going for it in their lives.

How would you like to die? Skydiving.

Phil Holcomb

Phil Holcomb was born in 1946 into an Army family and therefore grew up living throughout the United States and Europe. He graduated with a B.S. in Business Administration from the University of Arizona, where he majored in marketing, and stayed on to complete his studies in law and received his Juris Doctor.

Like his father, Mr. Holcomb joined the Army and served as an Army officer in Germany and Vietnam from 1966 - 1970. He later worked as a trial lawyer handling civil litigation in both Tucson, Arizona and Portland, Oregon.

Phil joined Context Associated in its formative years, starting in January of 1980. He served a variety of roles in the company, including vice president, and was the first person besides Randy Revell to lead its programs. After some years as a Program Leader, Phil returned to the practice of law. He rejoined Context in 1994 and is presently serving as Special Assistant to the President, a Program Leader, and San Francisco Area Director.

Phil Holcomb resides in San Francisco, and enjoys reading both fiction and non-fiction, watching films, and playing tennis.

Phil's story, "Sara and Her Juice" will strike a chord with anyone who has ever been a parent, or with anyone who is working on his relationship with himself.

It still works for Phil, too. To find out more about Phil and his relationship with himself, tune in to the answers below.

If you were cloned, what would your duplicate be doing right now? Relaxing with a good book on a warm and sunny beach.

Who or what makes you laugh loudest and longest? I make myself laugh the loudest and longest when I catch myself taking myself and my life too seriously.

What is your greatest extravagance? Picking up the tab.

What do you value most in your friends? Participation and humor.

What do you consider to be your greatest achievement? I haven't done it yet.

Which talent would you most like to have? To play a musical instrument—the piano or saxophone.

What is your primary leadership style? I'm a controller. I think it is a scream that my formal/reserved initial presentation of myself is so different from how I feel internally.

Who are your heroes in real life? Winston Churchill, Muhammed Ali, Martin Luther King, and my sister, Judy Revell.

What one world problem would you like to have the most impact on? Racial, ethnic and religious intolerance.

What does your personal life look like? I'm in a fairly new relationship. I am both excited and challenged by it and have a strong sense of the present and the future.

Are you funny at home? Do they like it? I am really funny and "they" like it to a point. I sometimes go too far.

How do you let off steam? Cry along with a good book or movie. Go for long walks. Sit in the sun.

What about your work keeps you coming back? The way I feel about me when I do it, and the reports of the successes of people I have encouraged.

How would you like to die? Quickly and privately.

Diane Kennedy

Diane Kennedy has a background in both early childhood education and adult education. She was born in Nova Scotia, where she taught school after receiving her teacher's certificate from Nova Scotia's Teacher's College. Diane then moved to Edmonton, Alberta, where she served as a kindergarten assistant for five years.

It was during her time in Edmonton, Alberta that Diane was introduced to Context Associated. She completed The Excellence Series in the fall of 1985, and started employment the next day as a marketing representative.

Diane and her family moved to Ottawa, Ontario in 1988. Diane attended her first humor conference in Saratoga Springs, New York that same year. What had started out as a hobby soon became a business, and Diane began giving workshops and seminars on such topics as: "Humor in the Workplace," "Humor in Healthcare," "Humor and Parenting," and "Increasing Your Joy in Life." She held workshops for the Federal Government and was keynote speaker for a variety of organizations, which led to a number of radio and television appearances.

Ms. Kennedy continued to volunteer for Context Associated, and returned to full-time employment in 1991 as Area Director for Ottawa. She won the company's Good Will Award for 1996.

Diane Kennedy is married with two grown children. She and her husband Ed enjoy family get-togethers and time spent outdoors, particularly visits to the ocean.

Diane Kennedy says when her time comes to die, she hope she goes out with her husband Ed, doing something wild and wacky! In the meantime, she was happy to share two of her most meaningful personal stories with us: "Laughter is The Best Medicine," and "Passing the Favor On." She managed to squeeze these answers out in between bursts of laughter.

If you were cloned, what would your duplicate be doing right now? Sipping piña coladas on the beach in Hawaii.

Who or what makes you laugh loudest and longest? Myself. Sometimes I'm just downright silly.

What is your idea of perfect happiness? Having close, intimate relationships with lots of fun and laughter, and making a huge contribution to people in my life as well as people yet unknown.

What is your greatest extravagance? Long-distance telephone calls!

What do you value most in your friends? I value their time and their caring.

What do you consider to be your greatest achievement? My 26-year marriage to the love of my life, my husband Ed.

What is your current fantasy about the future? That I get sexier as I get older. Hey - it's my fantasy, and I'm sticking to it!

What sport or piece of music does your life look like? I liken my life to a carousel ride at a carnival—always in motion, lots of ups and downs; sometimes smooth, sometimes an abrupt stop; but the motion always starts again.

What is your primary leadership style? Controller with a bit of promoter thrown in. My one-liners are hysterical, even if I'm the only one who gets them.

How do you keep it fresh? By adding Bounce, of course!

Who are your heroes in real life? My family. My mother for her fight against cancer. My dad for always being there. And my mother-in-law who was widowed early in life with three little children. She just quietly handled it all. I have a lot of respect and admiration for her.

What one world problem would you like to have the most impact on? Creating a stronger youth in our world—giving them hope and better choices in life.

What is your most treasured possession? My mother's diamond ring that she gave me just before she died. I never take it off.

Are you funny at home? Do they like it? Yes, I am very funny at home. They don't always understand it, but they say at least I'm not boring!

What is your motto? I always land on my feet.

What about your work keeps you coming back? Absolutely the people. I love people, and this is a people business.

Joanne Kotjan

Joanne Kotjan is part of the very heart and soul of Context Associated, since her first participation with the company in March of 1980.

Born and raised in Philadelphia, Joanne graduated from the University of Pittsburgh with a B.A. in Spanish, and received her M.A. in Comparative Literature from the University of Wisconsin. Next came a move to Chicago, where she worked with an educational agency that accredits programs in medical technology.

At the age of 26, Joanne bought a van and took her act on the road, landing in Seattle, Washington—a place she had seen once on a vacation "on 2 sunny days in September." As a Real Estate Broker and salesperson for 7 years, Joanne specialized in sales of recreational property, including one of the first timeshares ever sold in that state.

In March of 1982, Joanne Kotjan joined Context Associated as one of its first Marketing Representatives. During the next 5 years Joanne was a leader in sales and part of the office that produced the single largest program in the company's history, as well as generating more than half of the company's gross revenue at that time.

Ms. Kotjan joined the Implementation Team and became Context's Sales Specialist in 1987, in charge of sales staff orientation and training; and went on to become Vice President. Today Joanne is a project consultant retained by the company.

Joanne most enjoys country living with her partner, cats and gardens, as well as hiking and biking and reading.

Cultivating beauty in both flowers and people is one of Joanne Kotjan's strengths in life. Courage is another. Her moving story, "With a Little Help From My Friends," demonstrates both of these extraordinary traits.

Joanne was kind enough to answer these ridiculous questions for her adoring public.

If you were cloned, what would your duplicate be doing right now? My clone would be doing all the housework. She would be the wife I've always dreamed of having.

What makes you laugh loudest and longest? I'm embarrassed to admit this, but sitcoms make me laugh the loudest. They're so corny and I somehow find comfort in their predictability. When I was recovering from cancer, I would watch very old reruns on Nick at Night. I think they took me back to a simpler time and I laughed a lot.

What is your idea of perfect happiness? Perfect happiness is sleeping in with my four kitties just as the sun rises over Mt. Baker and the bay. It just doesn't get much better.

What is your greatest extravagance? Plants are my greatest extravagance—buying one of almost everything, even when we have no place to put it. We somehow make room and just keep digging more beds.

What do you value most in your friends? I value kindness, compassion and just hanging out together.

What do you consider to be your greatest achievement? Being the first female athlete in my high school to earn 10 varsity letters.

What is your current fantasy about the future? My fantasy about the future is that our world will truly honor and value diversity. I dream that soon we will see each other for who we really are and that the illusion of separation will be gone.

What is your primary leadership style? As an analyzer, loss of face is a fate worse than death. I have loved the times around Halloween when I donned a clown's costume and acted really silly. I just kept telling myself that no one knew it was me—HAH!

How do you keep it fresh? I know that my greatest challenge in life is to keep myself inspired. I work at allowing myself as much unstructured time as possible to do things "as the spirit moves me." I'm amazed and delighted at the ordinary and extraordinary places I go.

Who are your heroes in real life? Hillary Clinton, Oprah Winfrey, Maya Angelou, Chris Williamson, Jimmy Carter, Billy Crystal—to name a few.

What one world problem would you like to have the most impact on? Education.

What is your motto? My dad had a standard answer to the question: What are you going to do today? He'd always answer "as little as possible." I'd like to let that response be my guide on the weekends.

Carol LaCroix

Carol LaCroix was born in Oregon and currently resides in the Seattle area. The mother of two children (now grown), Carol is a high-energy, multi-talented and entertaining woman with a background in technical writing in the computer graphics industry and in management.

Carol excelled for a number of years as a family and crisis counselor for The Boys and Girls Aid Society of Oregon, a 100-year-old private, non-profit social service agency. Her unique ability to establish trust and rapport resulted in her working with the toughest of the "street kids" and juvenile offenders.

One of the original program leaders for Context Associated, Carol LaCroix has been a facilitator of human development and effectiveness courses for almost two decades. She is one of only a few program leaders who is trained and experienced in leading both business and general programs for Context Associated. She is also the principal leader of the company's youth programs.

The many thousands of students and clients who have attended courses conducted by Carol have particularly acknowledged that her highly developed listening skills, her knowledge and precise articulation of course materials, and her tremendous wit and sense of humor significantly enhanced their learning experiences.

Carol LaCroix is so full of personality, she has been likened to a force of nature. Attractive, vivacious, and intelligent, Carol leads a full and active life. She describes one unique experience in her life in her story "The Dolphins." She shares a few more carefully chosen words in her answers to the questions below.

If you were cloned, what would your duplicate be doing right now? Being a student someplace in the world.

Who or what makes you laugh? Robin Williams.

What is your greatest extravagance? Music, books, shoes and lipsticks.

What do you value most in your friends? A keen mind, a probing intellect, and a good sense of humor.

What do you consider your greatest achievement? Raising my family.

Which talent would you most like to have? I would love to dance like Baryshnikov, compose music like Beethoven, and use the written word to inspire.

What is your primary leadership style? I am a promoter. I sometimes listen to myself talking and find that I don't agree!

Who are your heroes in real life? The author and aviatrix, Beryl Markham. My dear friend Bob Martin, who was very bright and very present. He died last year.

What one world problem would you most like to have an impact on? Intolerance.

What about your work keeps you coming back? I find it interesting, and there are people here that I would really miss.

What is your motto? I like to use this quotation from George Bernard Shaw as advice for myself: "This is the true joy in life, the being used for a purpose recognized by yourself as a mighty one. I am of the opinion that my life belongs to the whole community, and as long as I live, it is my privilege to do for it whatever I can. I want to be thoroughly used up when I die, for the harder I work, the more I live. I rejoice in life for life's sake. Life is no "brief candle" to me. It is a sort of splendid torch which I have got hold of for the moment, and I want to make it burn as brightly as possible, before handing it on to future generations."

Pam Mason

Pam Mason grew up in Milton-Freewater, Oregon. She received her B.A. in English from the University of Oregon, and her M.A.T. in English from Portland State University. She taught high school English for 13 years, and participated with a group of teachers in writing a series of textbooks on how to teach writing.

After joining Context Associated as a marketing representative in 1987, she noticed an amazing difference in working with adults who were paying for their education! Pam has been the Area Director for the Portland, Oregon office since December of 1990.

Pam has been married for 15 years to her husband, Richard. She also enjoys the company of their dog, two grown step-children, and three grandsons. Her passions these days include travel, beautiful clothes, and weight-lifting.

In addition to the courses offered at Context Associated, Pam considers her marriage to be both a great achievement and a great avenue for learning. Pam says that "keeping a marriage going and growing has taken more commitment, perseverance, forgiveness (of myself and him), and acceptance than I ever thought possible." Her story, "The Learning Curve," represents some of her early learning in this area.

Pam agreed to indulge our curiosity by answering these questions.

What is your idea of perfect happiness? Being adored.

Who makes you laugh loudest and longest? What makes me laugh these days is my dog Beemer. He's a Bichon Frise. He has big black eyes and thinks he's human. Dog lovers say that bichons aren't dogs, they're cotton people. He gets playful and romps and pounces, and it's like the attack of the Q-Tip! He also gives me unconditional love—maybe there's a pattern here.

What are your greatest extravagances? Clothes and travel. Actually, they're my husband's greatest extravagances. I really picked well in the husband department! We love traveling, and going off the beaten paths to hang out with the locals. We have most enjoyed cruising the Caribbean, Costa Rica, Brazil and Mexico. We met in Hawaii, so the tropics really bring back those lovey-dovey feelings.

What do you value most in your friends? I most love my friends who let me be me, without expectation. That's challenging, since many people think that since I'm a Context employee, I should be "fixed." My true friends love me as I am, and in fact, many times give me more slack than I give myself.

What is your primary leadership style? I am a supporting controller. When I first found out that I was a controller, I didn't want my husband to know. Of course, in talking to him later I found out that I was the only person who wasn't okay with being a controller— every other person close to me had known and accepted it for years.

This exercise was important for me in another way. I had judgments about Richard, and why he always wanted so much attention. I thought some day he would "grow up" and be more like me. When I found out he was a promoter, it all made sense. I became much more accepting of him.

Who are your heroes in real life? My Dad died in December of 1995. Caring for him before his death was a life-changing experience for me. He was a strong, dignified man, and he is present in my heart.

My latest hero is my mother. She just turned 69, and is a recent graduate of our programs. She's young and forward thinking. She's a fabulous supporter; positive, loving and kind—willing most of the time to change her mind. Spontaneous. Those are all things I want to be when I'm her age.

What about your work keeps you coming back? One of the reasons I'm involved in the work we do is because I would love to see the world at peace in my lifetime. I want everyone to get along. My song is "Let There Be Peace On Earth, And Let It Begin With Me." The work we do, assisting each person to be at peace with herself, is the best way I know to begin.

Michele McNickle

Born in Hudson, New York, Michele McNickle moved to the state of Michigan at one and a half years of age. She received her B.A. in Advertising from Michigan State.

Prior to employment with Context Associated Michele was employed by Chase Manhattan Personal Financial Services, where she specialized in marketing and marketing research. She has also done freelance work in advertising.

Graduate Manager for the Context Associated's Seattle office from 1993 through March of 1997, Michele has been leading programs since 1993. She entered the Master's program at Antioch University in January of 1997, seeking a degree in Whole Systems Design. A relatively new field, Whole Systems Design takes a more holistic approach to human systems and organizations.

Michele is married and currently resides in Redmond, Washington.

Michele McNickle is the author of "Real Life." Her real life right now is extremely full—she leads programs full time, has just completed four years as Seattle's Graduate Manager and is working towards her Master's degree! In fact, that's probably why she and her clone headed off to the beach. Before she left, she gave us these answers.

If you were cloned, what would your duplicate be doing right now? She would already be starting my vacation on some sandy white beach in Mexico!

What is your idea of perfect happiness? To be feeling really good about myself, proud of my accomplishments, and madly in love with my husband on a sunny day.

What is your greatest extravagance? Spending the day in my hammock. Or champagne, strawberries and dark chocolate for dinner!

What do you value most in your friends? Their courage to be honest with me and with themselves.

What was your wildest, most dangerous or most unique experience? I'm not sure, but if I think of one, it's probably best not to put it in print!

What is your primary leadership style? I am a promoting controller. That means I can make myself laugh and tick myself off at the same time!

How do you keep it fresh? Remembering to take time to take care of me and posing new challenges to myself. I love variety!

Who are your heroes in real life? Teachers. Anyone willing to share their wisdom.

What one world problem would you like to have the most impact on? The misuse of power and leadership. If all people do not begin to value themselves, we're in big trouble.

What does your personal life look like? Right now it looks like a fraternity house!

What is your most treasured possession? My stuffed dog named Brutus. I found him in the attic at my grandmother's house when I was seven. He's about 35 years old, and he's had the fuzz loved off of him.

What sport or piece of music is your life most like? Volleyball. Sometimes it's a driving spike that wins the game, and sometimes it's the soft touch. And you can't play without other people on your team.

What is your motto? "I came here to live out loud." -- Emile Zola

Kate Menard

Kate Menard has been a champion laugh-producer for 43 years.

She received her B.A. degree in History from Queens University in Kingston, Ontario. Her 14-year career in hotel service in Toronto included reception and accounting duties. She also worked at the Southampton Princess Hotel in Bermuda for three years.

Kate was introduced to The Excellence Series in August of 1992 and joined Context Associated as Ontario's Operations Manager in March of 1993. She currently holds the position of Area Director for the Ontario Region.

In addition to swimming and laughing, Kate enjoys reading and hugging her dog.

The author of "Back in the Swim of Things," Kate has learned a lot about persistence and perseverance. Kate recently became a non-smoker when she realized that by the age of 65, she would have spent $86,000 on her habit. A month later she turned her savings into a new car!

Thanks to Kate's exquisite sense of humor, she graciously agreed to answer the following questions.

If you were cloned, what would your duplicate be doing right now? Enjoying life as I am.

Who or what makes your laugh loudest and longest? Life's absurd moments, puns and word play.

What is your idea of perfect happiness? Being beamed from place to place, instead of flying.

What do you value most in your friends? Acceptance, humor, proactivity.

What was your wildest, most dangerous or most unique experience? Living in Bermuda. Living with a film production company.

What do you consider to be your greatest achievement? Actually wanting to stay in one job for more than 4 years—this job.

What is your primary leadership style? Controlling promoter. I am crisp and laser-like (just like cereal.)

Who are your heroes in real life? Queen Elizabeth II and people who get it done without fanfare.

What one world problem would you like to have the most impact on? Literacy.

What is your most treasured possession? My car and my dog.

What does your personal life look like? Quiet, unstructured, messy, needing lots of space. My life resembles baseball—flurries of activity followed by periods of quiet.

What about your work keeps you coming back? Fun, chaos, freedom, results, people.

What is your motto? Screw 'em if they can't take a joke!

Gerri Moulton

Gerri Moulton is a woman with both a big heart and a big mission. She grew up in the suburbs of Montreal, where she attended business college with an emphasis on accounting. She spent the next 17 years in Ottawa in a variety of roles that included manager of a retail pharmacy outlet, and retail sales and management for bedroom furniture; while raising two wonderful daughters.

Introduced to Context Associated in 1982, Gerri joined the company in October of 1983 as a marketing representative. She accepted the position of Area Manager for Vancouver and surrounding areas in May of 1988, and became Regional Manager in September of 1990. Her area today includes British Columbia, Alberta, Saskatchewan, Manitoba and Hawaii. Ms. Moulton has been leading programs since 1987.

Gerri's favorite leisure-time pursuits are experimental cooking, reading, repositioning furniture, and walking on the beach or the seawall.

Gerri Moulton is a woman with a big vision, and a real love for her adopted homeland of Vancouver, British Columbia. Her story, "Seeing With My Heart," tells the story of her love for the mountains and oceans of her new home. Her other main love, these days, is her 6-year-old grandson, Rory.

We asked Gerri to respond to these highly personal and impertinent questions.

If you were cloned, what would your duplicate be doing right now? If I were cloned, my duplicate would be answering these questions!

Actually, we would be doing twice as much of the same things. I could be in two places at once helping out my areas more, and I would take more vacations.

Who or what makes you laugh loudest and longest? Watching children play or playing with them. Their laughter is infectious. Also animals at play make me laugh as well.

What is your idea of perfect happiness? Perfect happiness is being completely at peace with myself all the time.

What is your greatest extravagance? My home. I pay an outrageous amount of rent to live there.

What do you value most in your friends? I most value my friends' loyalty and honesty.

What was your wildest, most dangerous or most unique experience? It was at a ski area north of Montreal. A group of us had gone up in a chartered bus. Several of us were non-skiers and went along just for fun. Someone in our group knew of a restaurant/club on the other side of the hill, and decided the quickest route was walking across a single track train trestle, several hundred feet in the air over a small stream of water, way below. I have a terrible fear of high places. I was terrified. I was teased into doing it anyway. I didn't change my mind at all about high places.

My most unique experience was the birth of my first daughter, followed closely by assisting at the birth of a friend's baby.

What is your current fantasy about the future? That I will continue to do the work I do now, and that I will meet and fall in love with a tall, generous man who adores me and we will live together happily for the rest of our lives.

What is your primary leadership style? I am a controller. I also think it is very humorous to think I have control over anything.

What one world problem would you like to have the most impact on? War. In a small way, I see myself as impacting war now by working on my own self-acceptance and encouraging others to do the same. I believe that on a global scale, if we were all in full self-acceptance, there would be no conflict.

What is your most treasured possession? A photo album full of memories of early romances, big dreams, lots of hope. There are pictures of my children from the time they were babies. It brings memories of fun and play, and a sense that I can handle anything in my life.

What is your motto? If you want a job done right, hire an expert.

How do you let off steam? By finding someone to talk to who will not give me advice.

What about your work keeps you coming back? The challenge of getting it right and the acknowledgment when I do.

Bobby Ng

Bobby Ng brings a wealth of communication skills and experience to the courses he facilitates. He was a radio-television personality for over 30 years, starting at age 16 in Manila and continuing in Vancouver, B.C. and Edmonton, Alberta.

His educational background includes a B.A. and B.S. in Commerce with honors from De La Salle University in Manila. His body of work covers a broad spectrum from anchoring nationwide election coverage in the Philippines to interviewing the likes of John Wayne and Harry Belafonte.

Mr. Ng co-founded an advertising agency in Manila and served as Vice President and General Manager. The company, Atlas Resources and Management Group, has grown and expanded in the TV-radio industry, real estate development, and investments.

Bobby joined Context Associated as a Program Leader in October of 1993. In addition to his other careers, Bobby has hosted tours to Australia, New Zealand, the Orient, Kenya, the Caribbean, the Panama Canal, and New York. Now it is his pleasure to host guided tours of the inner self.

Commitment to quality results, sincerity, caring and humor are key characteristics of all the programs he leads.

Bobby, his wife Mary Lou, and their son Brent, make their home in Edmonton, Alberta. Living in the Vancouver area are Ron, with wife Dana and son Andy, and Chris—two sons from a previous marriage.

Between his wide range of careers in the international arena, and his dramatic experiences on-stage ("Counting On Time"), Bobby has certainly led a rich and full life. His other story, "Walking on Broken Glass," illustrates the value he has found in being clear about what is important in life, and committing to make it happen.

We were fortunate enough to catch Bobby in between plane trips, and he graciously consented to share these insights into his life and personality.

Who makes you laugh? These days, Jay Leno and Robin Williams.

What is your idea of perfect happiness? Enjoying the love, respect and companionship of those I love and admire, in an environment of fun—free from pressure, problems and worries.

What do you value most in your friends? Acceptance, respect, honesty, humor, intelligence, and loyalty.

What do you consider your greatest achievements? There are several. One was doing TV-radio play-by-play coverage of the top leagues of the Philippines' national sport, basketball, starting at the impressionable age of 17. My idols then were sports stars and sportscasters. I was also already covering special events, including the presidential election.

Then there was the memorable time I emceed two concerts by the Beatles. I talked with them on a few occasions and wrote it up in a series of articles for the front page of the leading newspaper in the Philippines.

What is your current fantasy about the future? The world is at peace. I am retired, with all the material things I need. I am enjoying my family and friends, traveling the world, and leading the occasional program.

What is your primary leadership style? I'm a controller. Often I'm so focused on what concerns me, I am insensitive to details. I've told my wife that if we're out together and she goes missing, I probably won't be able to tell police what she's wearing.

How do you keep it fresh? I keep learning something new, whether it be a piece of subject matter or a facilitating technique. And a whole new set of participants with their dreams, walls, personalities, histories, and problems goes a long way to keeping it fresh for me.

Who are your heroes in real life? In my younger days, my idols were Frank Sinatra, Humphrey Bogart, and Doris Day. But I'm afraid my days of hero worship are over. I do admire people who unselfishly give of themselves in the service of others.

What is your most treasured possession? Probably a souvenir program autographed by the Beatles. Yet, having said that, I'm not sure where I've placed it!

What is your personal life like? Are you funny at home? When not working, I spend one or two days a week being Mr. Mom to our son Brent. I catch up on sleep, mail bills, do errands, watch taped TV shows, and read. Sometimes I think I'm funny at home, but my wife Mary Lou may have a different perspective.

What is your motto? Aim High!

What about your work keeps you coming back? It fills every one of my driving needs.

Carol Peringer

Born in Bellingham, and raised in Kirkland, Washington, Carol Peringer has a varied background that includes business, education and family life. Carol is a serious student of life, and says that her wealth of experiences have earned her several "life degrees".

Ms. Peringer's work experiences include alternate education, employment with the phone company, and store manager for a successful clothing retailer in California. During her stay in California, Carol gave birth to two of her three children at home while living on a self-sufficient mini-farm, raising animals and growing food for her family.

Upon returning to her home state of Washington, she became a staff member of Natural High School, an alternative public school in which the curriculum and disciplinary systems were designed and implemented by staff and students alike. She also has experience in the stock brokerage business.

Carol's first position with Context Associated was as an assistant to the Vice President in charge of the Support Center. She began leading programs in 1986. After a 3 year hiatus in which she focused on her children, and purchased and restored a house; Carol returned in 1992 to lead programs full-time.

Ms. Peringer is married to a freelance artist/illustrator and is the mother of 3 children. She is an artist in her own right, creating bead jewelry and dolls out of her vast bead collection. She also enjoys reading and gardening.

Carol's love of family and friends is evident in her life and her work, and in her story "My Romance" as well. More of what Carol loves appears in her answers to the following questions.

Who or what makes you laugh loudest and longest? My friends Pam Mason and Kathleen Carie make me laugh long and loud. I love the experience of laughing hard, as I do when I am around the irreverent Ms. Carie.

I laugh at the absurdity of life. And when I'm camping in the summer with my husband and son, with nothing to focus on except being in the moment, then I notice a lot of funny things in life, I just crack up over nothing.

What is your idea of perfect happiness? I remember a great day in our cabin, when all three of my kids were there. It was the way they were interacting with each other, that they were in touch with the bond that we have together as a family. My kids, my husband, and I were all coming from a very loving place. It was a beautiful setting, with the people I care most about in this world. All was right in the world to me. That was my idea of perfect happiness.

What do you value most in your friends? Knowing that we're connected, knowing that we're in it together for life, that's really important to me.

What do you consider to be your greatest achievement? My relationships. Specifically, my kids, my family, my friends.

What was your most unique experience? A real highlight of my life was the birth of my granddaughter last fall. I was there supporting my daughter as she gave birth to her own daughter. It was a monumental event.

What is your most treasured possession? My family. Of material things, it would be my grandmother's ponytail. I have used pieces of her hair in the artwork I have created.

What is your primary leadership style? I am an analyzing promoter. I love to go into office supply stores to buy really cool tools and toys to organize my life. Then I take them home and forget why I bought them. They stay in the bag in a closet and I never use them.

What about your work keeps you coming back? The love in our programs. Our programs assist people in loving themselves, and teach the importance of loving others.

What is your motto? Love is all there is. That's my most important belief about life.

David Porter

David Porter is an enthusiastic and engaging person with a ready wit and a flair for the dramatic. He has a Masters Degree in Public Administration from the University of Washington, where he focused on human resource management and training.

His employment background includes a variety of career fields that cover economic development, marketing, business administration, and human resource management. He has been a small business owner, organizational development consultant, restaurant marketing director, and personnel manager. He is currently the Vice President of the Economic Development Council of Snohomish County, Washington.

David attended his first Context Associated course in August, 1979 and has been a long-time supporter of the company and its programs. He has been a Program Leader since January of 1996.

Born in New England and raised in Virginia, David moved to the Seattle area in 1971. He lives in Everett, Washington with his wife, Carol, and their three sons.

David shares his deep feelings about fatherhood in his story, "The Lion's Den", and calls his wife and children the real heroes in his life. Another hero and mentor, Chester the cat, appears in his story, "Sales: It's the Cat's Meow!"

David Porter shares his slightly askew take on life in these answers to some equally askew questions.

If you were cloned, what would your duplicate be doing right now? Eating scrambled eggs and raisins.

Who makes you laugh? The people on the original "Saturday Night Live."

What is your idea of perfect happiness? An abundant supply of oxygen.

What do you value most in your friends? Integrity and humor.

What was your wildest, most dangerous, or most unique experience? Having the airplane hit the top of my car while we were playing a game of chicken.

Which talent would you most like to have? To play the piano brilliantly by sight.

What is your primary leadership style? Controlling and authoritative. Participants get a kick out of my dressing up like General Patton on Sunday morning.

How do you keep it fresh? Airwick and dental floss.

What one world problem would you like to have the most impact on? The escalating salaries of professional sports personalities.

What is your motto? Rout dragons from their lairs.

What piece of music is your life most like? The "piece" of music I'm most attracted to is a treble clef. It has great lines, and always seems to capture the high notes.

How do you let off steam? White water rafting, chopping wood, Cuban cigars.

What about your work keeps you coming back? High drama, being the center of attention, contribution.

How would you like to die? From cardiac arrest caused by multiple orgasms at age 92 years.

Arlene Rannelli

Arlene Rannelli is a very intuitive, charming, insightful woman. She has a unique way of showing her respect for individuals and, as a result, there is an atmosphere of safety and trust in the programs she facilitates.

Born, raised and educated in Montreal, Quebec, Arlene received her license as a stockbroker with Greenshields Inc. in 1974. In 1980, Arlene and her young daughter moved to the Okanagan Valley where Arlene went on to obtain additional market-related licenses including life and disability insurance.

During her career as an Investment Advisor, Arlene taught many seminars as well as investment courses at Okanagan College. She has been a guest speaker at various Men's and Women's Clubs and also provided up-to-date stock market information on both radio and television in the Okanagan Valley.

Ms. Rannelli joined Context Associated in January of 1989 as a Marketing Representative, and began leading programs in June of 1992.

Arlene's passion for life, her enthusiasm, her warmth and her determination are an inspiration to many.

Arlene's story, "Asking the Right Questions," reflects what she feels is her greatest achievement—raising her daughter while being a single mom. Her greatest hope is that people all over the world will begin to choose love as their defining experience. In "Good Intentions," Arlene discusses one precept that may help in leading the way.

Arlene shares other aspects of her ideas and experiences in answering the following questions.

If you were cloned, what would your duplicate be doing right now? Teaching a spirituality course.

What is your idea of perfect happiness? Perfect happiness is feeling the heat of the sun on my body and feeling connected with God.

What do you value most in your friends? I value honesty.

What is your next big goal? To publish my book.

Which talent would you most like to have? To consistently say and do whatever is necessary each moment to influence people to take their next step immediately.

What is your primary leadership style? I'm a controller. Not much is humorous about controllers except when we think we are funny and another controller is laughing. (Not very many other people get it.)

How do you keep it fresh? I relate to the newness of the people who are attending, and I view each one as a person I want to influence to be more effective in their lives. That assists me in staying conscious about what I am saying, why I am saying it, and how it is delivered. I find that exciting.

Who are your heroes in real life? Each person who has the courage to break through their walls.

What one world problem would you like to have the most impact on? I would like to bring an end to fear.

What is your most treasured possession? My conscious mind.

What does your personal life look like? I live in what I consider to be a beautiful home with my husband (1994) and periodically with my daughter—both of whom I love with all my heart. I believe that I am extremely fortunate to have these two people in my life. I am totally honest with them, and we have fun together. I am not particularly funny, although we tend to laugh a lot together.

My husband and I golf together and share similar spiritual beliefs. We are a great support to one another. My daughter and I go to dinner together about twice a month and we really enjoy each other's company. She is also a controller, as is my husband, so we are all pretty driven.

What about your work keeps you coming back? The thought that I am making a difference in the lives of the people I come into contact with in a very positive way, and in a way that benefits the world.

Elisabeth Revell

Elisabeth Revell was born in 1968 in Fort Meade, Maryland, and spent much of her growing years in San Francisco, California. She returned to the east coast to attend Franklin & Marshall College, where she received her B.A. in 1990 as a Business Major with an English Minor.

Some of her many activities and accomplishments while at Franklin & Marshall College were: Captain of the Varsity Women's Crew Team, Senior Class Secretary/Treasurer, Founder and General Manager WFMC (Campus Television Station), Member of the Dean's Advisory Board, and student life intern.

Elisabeth received her M.B.A. from Villanova University in 1995, and was Founder and President of Villanova M.B.A. Student Association. She was concurrently employed by Environex, Inc. from 1990-1995, an International environmental consulting firm specializing in air pollution control technologies. Her titles there included: Office Manager (1990-1993) and Automobile Industry Project Specialist (1993-1995).

Ms. Revell joined Context Associated in San Francisco in 1995 as Special Projects Manager for 1995-1996. She was promoted to Chief Financial Officer in 1996, and was on the design and implementation team for Context Associated's first EXPO held in March, 1997.

Elisabeth Revell enjoys a variety of hobbies and interests: creating stained glass, rollerblading, reading, and music. She is a volunteer for alumni organizations in fundraising and recruitment.

Elisabeth Revell is the author of "Tradition," a warm and affectionate look at her family life; and "The Magic Chuckle," the beginning of taking on a life of her own. Having attended all the programs herself as a participant, she recalls a special moment in Mastery "when my father was my program leader. I was speaking in front of the room, and I said something that I had never articulated to him (or to anyone else) before, but I could see by his reaction that he already knew it about me. I could see how close we are, and knew we were getting even closer."

Elisabeth brings her forthright and quietly elegant style to these rather vague and inelegant questions.

If you were cloned, what would your duplicate be doing right now? Something artistic.

Who makes you laugh? Eddie Murphy.

What is your idea of perfect happiness? Being involved with people and projects that grow and improve as a result of my involvement.

What is your greatest extravagance? Time I spend puttering around my apartment with no real purpose.

What do you value most in your friends? Inclusion, caring and acceptance.

What was your wildest, most dangerous or most unique experience? I traveled for a month through Europe by myself with not much of a plan.

What do you consider to be your greatest achievement? Following my own life path, doing what I considered most important to me along the way, despite great internal and external pressure to change course. Being happy with where I ended up.

What is your current fantasy about the future? To get married and have children. To be surrounded by friends and family. To have many areas of my life where I am helping things and people improve and grow. That Context Associated grows to be strong and wildly successful.

Who are your heroes in real life? My biggest heroes are people who have the willingness, insight and energy to adapt to the times such that they can do what they love and keep making a contribution. An example is Tina Turner. Another example is the two people who have influenced me most in my life, my wonderful parents (equally).

What one world problem would you like to have the most impact on? Pessimism.

What does your personal life look like? Are you funny at home? I am very optimistic. I am fairly quiet. Sometimes I am funny, but it is rare, unexpected, expressive humor.

My favorite times are sitting around with great friends and/or family with a bottle of good wine, good food, good music and good conversation.

What is your motto? How can I make this better?

Judy Revell

Judy Revell was born in Sacramento, California. Via the U.S. Army, Judy and her brother, Phil, moved with their parents all over the United States and Germany.

Judy began her college years at The University of Maryland at Munich, Germany and continued at George Mason University in Arlington, Virginia and Mary Washington College in Fredericksburg, Virginia. She earned a B.A. in History and received her teaching certificate in secondary education.

After college, Judy met Randy Revell while he was serving in the U.S. Air Force. He was assigned to the National Security Agency in Ft. Meade, Maryland when they were married in September of 1965. Judy sold advertising space for The Green Book (the social register of Washington, D.C.) as well as worked as a substitute teacher. In love with the idea of possibility, she then became a stockbroker in Washington, D.C.

In 1968 Judy's daughter Elisabeth was born, and the family moved to California later that year. Here the Revells became increasingly involved in the field of human possibility. Together Judy and Randy Revell designed and incorporated Context Associated in 1978.

Judy Revell served as Chief Financial Officer from Context's inception until her stroke in 1991. She now contributes through the company's weekly newsletter.

Judy Revell personifies "Faith That Moves Mountains." She is equally well known as a woman of great dignity, elegance and grace as well as one who loves mental stimulation, is deeply interested in everyone and everything, and enjoys laughing until she cries. The author of "A Woman's Right" and "When You Wish Upon A Star", Judy offers us this peek at the private side of a public life by answering the following questions.

Who or what makes you laugh? I laugh when I find joy in what someone says or does. Although it's harder, I usually find joy in my current situation.

What is your idea of perfect happiness? I have lots of answers to that. One thing I know is I am happy when I find joy.

What is your greatest extravagance? Context Associated. But it's not "extra", as implied by the word extravagance. Context Associated is most of my life, if not my whole life.

What do you value most in your friends? The ability to find joy in all circumstances, and being accustomed to success.

What was your wildest, most dangerous or most unique experience? Looking back, I think it was agreeing to marry someone after only three dates, and following through with it in slightly more than three months.

What do you consider to be your greatest achievement? I find this question extremely difficult to answer, even though achievement is one of the top elements in my Definition of Success. Philosophically speaking, we are always achieving.

I am proud of my husband and daughter and their achievements. Their attitudes and behaviors exemplify the traits of succeeding, finding joy, and living life with a "can do" attitude that I admire.

What is your next big goal? To have Context Associated be better known.

Which talent would you most like to have? This must sound strange in a book filled with stories by people who earn their living speaking in public ... it's public speaking that I would like to develop. I shake just at the thought of addressing a crowd. I have led seminars, but shakily. So far developing my public speaking is a wish, because I haven't taken the necessary action steps.

What about your work keeps you coming back? It's people and their "can do" attitude.

What is your motto? Now it's "One step at a time." Underlying that is "Yes I can."

Randy Revell

Randy Revell is not only an outstanding leader and innovator in the field of self-awareness, but he is also a warm and exciting person who is intensely interested in, and constantly studying, all aspects of human potential and motivation.

He holds a B.S. degree in Electrical Engineering from the University of Wyoming and has done postgraduate work in mathematics and communications at American University in Washington, DC. His eleven years with the U.S. Government include duty as an instructor of electronics, an educational television program producer, Captain in the U.S. Air Force, and over five years with the National Security Agency in communications.

Randy has had multi-faceted experiences which have contributed to his extensive knowledge of business and people. He formed the first "restaurant club" in the United States, did a stint as a venture capitalist in California's Silicon Valley, served as a consultant to top management of a number of Fortune 500 companies, and was involved with several training companies. He co-founded Context Associated late in 1978.

One of Randy Revell's most unique qualities is his ability to apply his experience and knowledge to his personal life as well as to his professional life. His activities over the past years have led to financial, professional and personal success. He knows from his own experience that his ideas about abundance and effectiveness work for people.

Mr. Revell currently resides in San Francisco with his wife Judy.

Anybody who has ever met Randy Revell has experienced his curiosity, his willingness to be fully engaged, and his deep love of people. It is no wonder, then, that these are some of the attributes of the lifelong learner described in his introductory essay, "Green and Growing." Randy also shares a very personal story from his childhood called "The White Feather Award," which foretells his calling to be a Champion of Good Will.

He brought his curiosity, love of people and sense of fun with him when answering these questions.

Who or what makes you laugh? The ridiculousness of the human condition. I laugh most at myself, particularly when I get to thinking that what I want is different from what I have.

I love people and usually end up in deep belly laughter during a spirited conversation.

What is your idea of perfect happiness? I know it is trite, but the good old days are here now. I strive to keep that in consciousness. This place, here, now, is the best there is for me—now.

What was your wildest, most dangerous or most unique experience? I've had several near-death experiences—all involving water—sailing, rafting, and scuba diving. These were earlier in my life when I lived closer to the physical edge. I'm less attracted to that now.

How do you let off steam? I treasure my hour on the treadmill every morning. Those endorphins are a very important part of my life.

What do you consider to be your greatest achievement? Being the best father I know how to be.

What novel, film or person has influenced you the most? The Bible most of all. Ayn Rand's "Atlas Shrugged" is a close second.

What is your primary leadership style? I'm all over the map.

I think my curiosity is one of my greatest strengths. The saying "curiosity killed the cat" has much meaning for me. In the program room I am always reining in my curiosity so I won't be disrespectful of a participant and violate his or her space.

Another important element in my Definition of Success is the experience of edge—that raw, sharp, fresh, alive feeling in the presence of threat. You can imagine how much tempering I do.

Who are your heroes in real life? Douglas Mac Arthur is one. His famous line, "I shall return" still moves me. I am impressed by his willingness to take a stand and deliver on it. People who deliver on their word in challenging circumstances get my attention.

What one world problem would you like to have the most impact on? Strengthening good will. That's what I'm about. The more good will that exists in a relationship, the safer it is for people. The more safety, the more willing people are to show up as they are, rather than as they think the other wants them to be. It is from this authenticity that miracles happen.

What does your personal life look like? Judy and I were married September 11, 1965. Our daughter, Elisabeth, was born March 4, 1968. My office has been in my home on and off for the past twenty years. We know most of our neighbors.

I believe one of the keys to rich relationships is to have mutual games (common areas of participation) to play. Context Associated is a game that Judy, Elisabeth and I get to play together. That is fun!

What is your motto? The first thing that comes to mind is the Golden Rule—Treat others as you would be treated. Most of my life I have honored this standard. The times when I haven't I consider breaches of integrity, and my great failures.

Another motto is that we all deserve respect. We deserve this for being, not for any awards we have won or contribution we have made.

What sport or piece of music is your life most like? My favorite song is "Amazing Grace." I think it is the theme of redemption that most moves me. Judy and I both love rags to riches stories—people fighting together to overcome difficult obstacles.

What about your work keeps you coming back? Through Context Associated we are making an incredible contribution to people's lives. It is this experience of contribution through strengthening good will that keeps me stepping up.

How would you like to die? Quickly, peacefully, and with a strong sense of contentment. I have no fear of death.

Mardig Sheridan

Mardig is truly the man with a thousand faces—and he has a career to go with each one of them! He performed with the musical group "The Bards" in the 1960's, and owned an advertising agency in the 1970's.

Mr. Sheridan established Mardig & Company, Inc. in 1982, where he acts as film producer and director as well as President and owner. He also writes, produces and directs commercials for radio and television. In addition, Mardig is a partner in Screamin' End Features, Inc., a management and production company for musical artists. Mardig and his partner are developing a major motion picture entitled "Be Bop A Lula."

Mardig started to mix his already expansive career activities with seminar facilitation in 1991. As a Program Leader for Context Associated, Mardig brings his incredible energy, sharp humor, and wealth of life experiences to his facilitation.

He is married to Stacey Sheridan, the love of his life and his best friend. He has two exceptional daughters, two rascal grandsons and two worthless cats. He enjoys cooking, working out, and golf; and is devoted to his home to such a degree that he actually enjoys yard work.

Creativity, humor and autonomy are his greatest strengths. If he tells you something will be done—it will be.

Mardig Sheridan's story, "The Pamper Pole," is just one of many dramatic and sensational stories of a man who likes to live large. Mardig says his life looks like a tennis match, and sounds like the music of Willie and Lobo. Despite his "rock star" resemblance, Mardig's heroes are his parents, and says his greatest achievement in life is his marriage to his wife, Stacey.

More about this vibrant personality and human tornado are revealed in the questions and answers that follow.

If you were cloned, what would your duplicate be doing right now? A real job paying lots of money.

What is your idea of perfect happiness? A Mexican beach any time of day.

What do value most in your friends? Humor and tolerance of me.

What is your next big goal? Writing another screenplay.

What is your current fantasy about the future? That I will have one.

Which talent would you most like to have? Invisibility.

What is your primary leadership style? Promoter. Note the five simultaneous careers.

How do you keep it fresh? My five simultaneous careers!

What does your personal life look like? Chaotic passion.

What is your motto? Begin with the end in mind.

How do you let off steam? In bursts.

What one world problem would you like to have the most impact on? Hatred.

What about your work keeps you coming back? The humor.

How would you like to die? Without warning.

Brenda Sorensen

Responsibility is one of the key characteristics of Brenda Sorensen. She began her career as a Dental Lab Technician while still in high school, and worked her way through college making teeth! Brenda completed her undergraduate degree in Architecture at the University of Washington, and continues to use her passion and skill in design to remodel a variety of homes.

Brenda has been a tops Sales Representative for Context Associated since 1984. In addition, she shares her extensive knowledge and experience in building and maintaining effective personal and professional relationships in the seminar, "Adventures in Intimacy."

Married for ten years to her best friend, seminar co-leader, and husband, Jim Sorensen, Brenda balances her love for her work with her love for family life. Daughter Katelyn is presently seven and a half years old, and was born at home. The Sorensens live in the Seattle area and enjoy spending time together, laughing a lot, tropical vacations, house renovations and immersing themselves in new ideas and experiences.

Readers of Brenda's story, "Raising A Magical Child," will understand why Katelyn Sorensen is the apple of her mother's eye. More about Brenda's interests and family life appear below.

If you were cloned, what would your duplicate be doing right now? All my responsibilities so I could play.

Who or what makes you laugh loudest or longest? My husband and daughter. We have a lot of fun together.

What is your idea of perfect happiness? Vacationing in the tropics with my husband and daughter ... relaxed, warm and tanned.

What is your greatest extravagance? Pampering. I love to have massages and other decadent things to pamper myself.

What do you value most in your friends? Integrity and honesty.

What was your wildest, most dangerous or most unique experience? I lived a pretty safe and sane life until I met my husband. He loves adventure. I've done more wild and adventurous things since we've been married than in my entire life before that.

What is your next big goal? To get some land out in the tulles, away from the city, with lots of space, nature, and trees. My family and I would enjoy more leisure time, and live a more simplified life together.

Which talent would you most like to have? To be able to clone myself.

What is your primary leadership style? I am an analyzer. I think being an analyzer is tough. I'm always thinking, figuring things out, watching, worrying, and weighing my decisions. It's exhausting.

What is your most treasured possession? My family. My family is my highest priority. I treasure the quality of my marriage and my bond with my daughter.

How do you keep it fresh? I continue growing, learning and striving. I love interesting and unique houses. Every home we have ever lived in has gone through different degrees of remodeling. Jim and I share an interest in alternative medicines and diet, and I have recently been studying Native American spirituality.

What one world problem would you like to have the most impact on? My wish is for people to see the earth as a living entity to be respected, cherished, honored, and healed; and for people to feel their connection to the earth and each other, and live more harmoniously, with love and appreciation.

What is your motto? Later!

What about your work keeps you coming back? I'm good at it, and there's nothing else I'd rather do for a living than making a difference in the world.

Jim Sorensen

Jim Sorensen is an artist, an entertainer, a teacher, a world traveler, and a dedicated family man. One of his most unique occupations was that of a scrimshander—an artist who creates detailed illustrations on fossilized mastodon ivory. He has written and illustrated several children's books, for which he was interviewed on NBC's After News Special.

As senior facilitator and Director of Training for Context Associated, Jim's realm of experience includes management, program design and program facilitation. Since joining the company in 1981, Jim has been instrumental in designing and implementing the company's sales system, staff training and compensation, area management and program innovations.

Jim genuinely enjoys what he does. He speaks year round both nationally and internationally to various organizations, businesses and government agencies. In his sixteen years of public speaking, Jim has been interviewed on over fifty talk shows. He had dedicated his career to assisting people in getting better results while increasing their level of personal satisfaction. His engaging and entertaining style has enlightened the lives of hundreds of thousands of those who have attended his presentations.

Jim Sorensen enjoys traveling to exotic locales, collecting unusual art and live specimens, and is an accomplished artist and illustrator with seven books to his credit. A devoted father and husband, Jim currently lives with his wife and daughter in Seattle, Washington.

Jim loves new places and experiences. Until moving to Seattle in 1980, the longest he had ever lived in one place was two and one half years (and that was in Viet Nam, during the war). He and his wife Brenda recently made his dream of living on a lake come true, when they bought a cute bungalow on a small lake north of Seattle. His story, "Dry Rot," is about remodeling this house. Jim also shares a humorous look back at the beginning of his career in public speaking with his story,

"Scared Spitless." More unusual, but truthful, information about Jim is revealed below.

Who or what makes you laugh? The unexpected, spontaneous humor of a situation. I love to tease people I care about. It's important to me to make life fun and to keep things simple.

What is your most treasured possession? An art deco bronze of Icharus that I fell in love with at an antiques store. I knew I couldn't afford it, so I walked in and out of that store several times debating with myself—the really cheap, common sense parts of me versus the part of me that really wanted it. The part of me that really wanted it won.

I collect other unusual things, including a collection of "open mouth" figurines and a collection of large, unique insects from around the world. (It took my wife a while to get comfortable with this collection.)

What is your greatest extravagance? I have traveled extensively and love taking exotic, adventurous vacations with my family. I like bringing back live souvenirs from my snorkeling adventures for my salt water aquarium.

What is your idea of perfect happiness? Snuggling with my wife and daughter, talking about happy stuff.

What do you consider to be your greatest achievement? Without a doubt it would be my marriage. I went from an infatuation vampire to a very happy, very committed married man.

And I love being a dad. One of my important priorities each week is to spend a morning helping out in my daughter's classroom. (I've been doing it since she was in kindergarten.) I have a huge respect for teachers and for the job they do.

What about your work keeps you coming back? The personal learning from working with such a variety of people in such a variety of situations.

Brent Stewart

Brent Stewart joined Context Associated as a Program Leader in April of 1992, after ten successful years in sales and management. His experience included handling major accounts for Xerox, and a variety of management positions, including general manager of an ice cream company. While at Xerox, Brent won several awards for his corporate presentation skills and he went on to become an award-winning Toastmaster as well as a public speaker on environmental issues.

Brent originally studied to be a teacher. He has a B.A. in English Literature and a Professional Teaching Certificate. He also has a background in music and theater, including a one year stint in a professional music/theater group. While at university, Brent incorporated his own company that proved so successful he ultimately moved to a career in the business world.

One of Brent's key interests is in health through diet and other natural means. He loves exercise and the outdoors and has a home in the Gulf Islands where he can "hear the silence." Brent has recently joined the management of Saje, a company which creates aromatherapy products and botanical remedies.

Brent takes his emotional well-being as seriously as he does his physical well-being. He talks about his quest for wellness in "Whose Problem Is It, Anyway?" and "A Hot Time in the Hot Tub Tonight!"

Brent agreed to leave his new hot tub long enough to answer these questions.

If you were cloned, what would your duplicate be doing right now? Lobbying against cloning.

What makes you laugh? Absurdity said with a straight face.

What is your idea of perfect happiness? A hammock for two, a tropical breeze, and an unlimited supply of avocados.

What is your greatest extravagance? Putting organic flax seed oil on my popcorn.

What do you value most in your friends? Intelligence. And ownership of a sailboat.

What was your wildest, most dangerous or most unique experience? Climbing a mountain in the Scottish Highlands, alone, in bad weather, searching for a Celtic Abominable Snowman.

What is your greatest achievement? Performing with an accapella group at the Queen Elizabeth Theatre in Vancouver, to a standing ovation.

What is your primary leadership style? I am a controlling analyzer. I add things I've already done to my "to do" list just so I can cross them off.

Who are your heroes in real life? John Robbins, Gandhi, Albert Schweitzer, Dr. Neil Bernard.

What one world problem would you most like to impact? Overpopulation.

What does your personal life look like? Quiet, rural. We live on an island.

Are you funny at home? Do they like it? We laugh a lot and we both like it.

What is your motto? All is well.
How would you like to die? Gracefully.

Dan Sullivan

Dan Sullivan is a native Washingtonian. His education includes a B.M.E. degree in Mechanical Engineering from Seattle University, and numerous post-graduate courses in business management.

His 17 years of professional and technical experience includes 13 years of direct management responsibilities in manufacturing and operations. He has worked for a variety of companies including Boeing and Coors Porcelain.

Dan began his career with Context Associated in July of 1985 as a marketing representative and was named top representative in the company for two years. He began leading programs in 1987 and has been leading programs full time since 1989. In 1993, Mr. Sullivan became Sales Manager of the Seattle area, the largest and most profitable operation in the company. Dan was appointed Director of Corporate Sales in 1996. He combines his experience in sales, sales management and program facilitation to provide an exceptional resource to clients of Context Associated.

Dan Sullivan currently lives on Vashon Island in Washington State, where he is active as an outdoor sports enthusiast. Dan enjoys skiing, backpacking and bicycling.

Although Dan says his heroes in real life are people who are themselves, it is Dan who is a hero to people at

Context Associated. Maybe it is because he exemplifies commitment and a willingness to do whatever it takes, two qualities displayed in his story, "A Second Chance."

We gave Dan a chance to answer these questions, and here are his responses.

If you were cloned, what would your duplicate be doing right now? The lawn.

Who or what makes you laugh the loudest and the longest? Clever, quick humor.

What is your idea of perfect happiness? An inner sense of peace and serenity.

What do you value most in your friends? Humor, integrity, loyalty.

What was your wildest, most dangerous or most unique experience? Being cloned.

What is your greatest achievement? Creating success from back to back crisis.

What is your primary leadership style? I'm an analyzer. I am waiting for "Consumer Reports, the Movie" to come out.

What one world problem would you like to have the most impact on? The environment.

What is your most treasured possession? My health.

What is your motto? Never answer stupid questions.

What sport is your life most like? Croquet: greener pastures and hard knocks.

What about your work keeps you coming back? Debt.

How would you like to die? I'd rather my clone died.

Trish van Vianen

Trish van Vianen describes herself as an "all around Canadian girl" due to the fact that she competed in figure skating, was a member of a provincial award-winning girls' curling team, and attended Girl Guides in her youth. She was born in northern British Columbia, and attended school in Prince George. She finished her training in the field of laboratory technology at the Southern Alberta Institute of Technology and worked as a Chemical Technologist for a hydrogen peroxide plant.

Returning to Prince George in 1988, Trish joined Context Associated as an Area Coordinator. She began leading programs in 1991.

Trish's current passions include: exploring the world with her children (aged 6, 7 and 14); enjoying skiing, camping, hiking, theater and baseball with her family; holding dinner parties with friends; and cramming as much adventure travel as possible into her full schedule.

When Trish says adventure and high drama, she really means it! After escaping from her backyard, (see "Don't Fence Me In"), Trish discovered excitement aplenty in Kathmandhu and surroundings. Just traveling one of Nepal's few paved roads along the mountain cliffs is an opportunity for pulse-racing, heart-stopping action!

When Trish caught her breath from her latest adventure, she answered these questions.

If you were cloned, what would your duplicate be doing right now? If I was cloned, my duplicate would be doing all the details in my life: housework, laundry, cooking, filing, etc. This would leave me free to play, go to the park, talk on the phone, drink wine with friends, ride my mountain bike with the kids.

Who or what makes you laugh loudest and longest? I love slapstick comedy, Robin Williams is incredible, and when people tease me or themselves from a place of good will, I laugh a lot! When a situation is difficult, and someone can point me in the direction of the humor in it, I laugh a lot. I also laugh at the funny antics of kittens and babies in discovery.

What is your idea of perfect happiness? Perfect happiness is having a sense of humor, lots of adventure, a large family and group of friends, plus facing my fear and doing it anyway.

What person or persons have influenced you the most? The Dalai Lama, Ghandi and Robin Williams have all influenced me. I admire their commitment to their core beliefs.

What is your current fantasy about the future? That I won't face any hardship I can't handle, that my children will lead happy, rich, full lives and live to be very old; that I will be very, very wealthy, and that I will have a relationship that has a very strong heartfelt connection.

What is your primary leadership style? I am a promoter. I love to start things. I've had the tendency to be involved with a new project, then a friend would phone and ask if I would go traveling with them. More often than not, I'd say yes, and no one would know where I was!

How do you keep it fresh? I keep my facilitation fresh by adding more of myself, using something I've just learned in my own life; but most of all, by connecting with the people.

Who are your heroes in real life? My heroes are people who don't have excuses for doing what they love to do.

What world problem would you most like to have impact on? Sanitation and illiteracy.

What does your personal life look like? Are you funny at home? My personal life is very busy. I am not a morning person, so I usually stagger around with a cup of coffee. I tend not to be funny at home, however, as the years go by, I am funnier and they do like it when I am that way. I am the organizer, I ensure that everything gets handled.

What is your motto? Do your best in every situation. Love your neighbor.

Mara Vizzutti

Mara's first language was Italian, even though she was born a "Calgary Cowgirl" in Alberta, Canada in 1964. She graduated from the University of Calgary with a degree in English Literature and a minor in Physical Education.

A jack of many trades, Mara has taught both junior and senior high school, sold advertising for a local arts magazine, as well as having been a fitness instructor. She began her career with Context Associated as a marketing representative, and has just recently completed her training as a Program Leader.

Among Mara's many pleasures and interests in life are horses, camping in the mountains, meditation, candles, hot tubs, marathons and mornings. Her passion for travel, especially to France, borders on addiction and affliction.

Mara may like marathons .... Besides being "Up Against the Wall," Mara uses running and swimming to let off steam. She also likes to paint.

She agreed to answer these questions when she came up for air.

Who makes you laugh? Dom DeLuise.

What is your idea of perfect happiness? An intimate connection with a loved one.

What is your greatest extravagance? Keeping my bathroom well stocked with scented body lotions and perfumes.

What do you value most in a friend? Loyalty, confidentiality, trust.

What was your wildest, most dangerous, or most unique experience? Sailing, motorcycling, convertible racing, a train ride, and flying over Venice in a Cessna—all in the same day!

What is your next big goal? Contribution on a larger scale, especially internationally.

What is your current fantasy about the future? Viewing the earth from space.

What talent would you most like to have? To be able to sing and play classical piano.

What is your primary leadership style? Promoting controller—I go from extreme focus to no focus to self-gratification NOW.

What one world problem would you like to have the most impact on? World peace.

What is your most treasured possession? My dishwasher!

What does your personal life look like? At home, I think walking around naked is good. I like talking to myself. My nest is just in its evolution—it's a new home.

What about your work keeps you coming back? The people, the contribution, the creation of community.

What is your motto? We're here for a good time, not a long time.

RESOURCES

CONTEXT ASSOCIATED MISSION

The mission of Context Associated is to strengthen, through our commitment to life long learning, the fabric of good will that exists in the world.

We are in the business of designing, selling and delivering educational opportunities for those seeking to enhance the quality of their personal and professional lives.

We believe that the more people know themselves, understand what is important to them and manifest this in their lives, the more good will is created and expanded.

All that we do has practical application, displays respect for the individual, enhances the relationship we have with one another and is filled with good humor.

We succeed as a result of an unwavering commitment to quality in our products and services. Quality is assured by team work, customer responsiveness, innovative marketing and the right use of resources.

Context Associated has offices throughout the world. Call for the location of an office nearest you. The central office is located at 3851 Clay Street, San Francisco, California 94118. (415) 387-7750

For more information and the location of an office near you, visit our web site at:

http://www.contextassociated.com

Order Form

Fax orders: (415) 387-7753

Telephone orders: Call Toll Free: 1 (888) 773-8355. Have
your AMEX, Discover, VISA or MasterCard ready.

On-line orders: webmaster@contextassociated.com

Postal orders: Context Associated, 3851 Clay Street, San
Francisco, CA 94118-1615, USA   Tel: (415) 387-7750

Please send _____ **copies of** *Moments of Truth:*
Personal Stories of Discovery.

Taxes:
Please add 7.75% sales tax for books shipped to
California addresses and 7% G.S.T. for books shipped to
Canadian addresses.

Shipping:
$4.00 for the first book and $2.00 for each additional
book.

Payment:
☐   Cheque
☐   VISA, ☐ MasterCard, ☐ AMEX, ☐ Discover

Card number: _____

Name on card: _____

Exp. date: _____ / _____

Call *toll free* and order now

Order   Form

Fax orders: (415) 387-7753

Telephone orders: Call Toll Free: 1 (888) 773-8355. Have
your AMEX, Discover, VISA or MasterCard ready.

On-line orders: webmaster@contextassociated.com

Postal orders: Context Associated, 3851 Clay Street, San
Francisco, CA 94118-1615, USA   Tel: (415) 387-7750

**Please send _____ copies of *Moments of Truth:
Personal Stories of Discovery.***

Taxes:
Please add 7.75% sales tax for books shipped to
California addresses and 7% G.S.T. for books shipped to
Canadian addresses.

Shipping:
$4.00 for the first book and $2.00 for each additional
book.

Payment:
☐   Cheque
☐   VISA, ☐ MasterCard, ☐ AMEX, ☐ Discover

Card number: _____

Name on card: _____

Exp. date: _____ / _____

Call *toll free* and order now